With an Outstretched Arm

A memoir of love and loss, family and faith

B.J. Yudelson

BenYehuda Press
Teaneck, New Jersey

Published by Ben Yehuda Press
122 Ayers Court Suite 1B
Teaneck, NJ 07666

http://www.BenYehudaPress.com

Ben Yehuda Press books may be purchased for educational, business, or sales promotional use. For information, please contact:
Special Markets, Ben Yehuda Press,
122 Ayers Court Suite 1B, Teaneck, NJ 07666
markets@BenYehudaPress.com

ISBN13 978-1-934730-41-6

The following chapters or portions of chapters have appeared previously in slightly different form:

Chapter 42: "The Simple Truth," *The Griffin*, 2011. Reprinted in *Longest Hours – Thoughts While Waiting*. 2013, Silver Boomer Press.

Chapter 72. "Dad's Last Thanksgiving," *A Quilt of Holidays: Stories, Poetry, Memoir*. 2012, Silver Boomer Press.

Chapter 75. "A Family Seder," *A Quilt of Holidays: Stories, Poetry, Memoir.* 2012, Silver Boomer Press.

13 14 15 / 10 9 8 7 6 5 4 3 2 20141115

To Larry and Miriam, and in memory of Ruth,
my children, who often led the way.

To Julian, my life partner,
who frequently objected but never held me back.

To my grandchildren: Yael, Ariella, Sam, Leah, Kinneret, Aviva, Joey, Ruthie, and Calanit.
May you each continue the quest for the Judaism that inspires you to live a full and righteous life.

1

It is 1977. We begin our Passover seder by singing the order of the rituals to come. We recite kiddush to bless the first cup of wine. We dip greens into salt water. Just as Julian says, "Let all who are hungry come and eat," there is a knock at the door.

"Who's there?" I call, trying to sound natural.

Besides my own family, our guests are two families who were our closest friends in the city where we used to live. Had they wondered about our middle child's absence?

The door opens. Ruth, at 10 a budding actress, steps in, a bandana on a stick slung hobo-style over one shoulder. "A poor and tired Jew."

"Where are you coming from?"

"Mitzrayim," *Egypt. The word* "Mitzrayim" *is related to the Hebrew word for narrow, constricted. I am grateful that Ruth is no longer constricted by fear, no longer the child afraid to put crayon to paper lest the result not resemble what she had in mind.*

"Where are you going?"

"Yerushalayim." *Jerusalem, the city of* shalom, *peace. Indeed, Ruth is blossoming into a self-confident child at peace with herself.*

"And what are you carrying?"

"Matzah..."

Amid adult smiles and a little friendly teasing by the children, Ruth takes her seat.

"Where'd you come up with that?" asks a guest.

"I read about it recently," I explain. "It's a standard part of the seder in Bukhara and other exotic places. I had no idea of all the places that Jews live."

Our family's seders tend to be long, full of questions and discussion, and conducted in a combination of Hebrew and English using a variety of Haggadot, *books that contain the text of this central ritual of Jewish life. While Ruth helped me in the kitchen in the days preceding Passover, I had told her about this custom.*

"Let's do it, Mom! It'll make our second seder, with all the same guests, different from our first."

As we had hoped, our little drama enlivens and inspires the evening's conversation.

So different, I think, from the seders I grew up with. Not that I hadn't loved them—I had—but we had followed a single, abbreviated Haggadah *with virtually no discussion. As I recall, my family had never probed the text's deeper meanings, had never explored connections with the worldwide Jewish community. My childhood seders were ritualized commemorations of the exodus from Egypt as the end of the slavery of our ancestors; our current seders are vibrant celebrations of the Exodus as the passageway into 3,000 years of Jewish life.*

* * *

I fastened my seat belt, and even before the flight attendant began her safety spiel, I opened the book I had grabbed on my way out the door. I planned to leaf through *The Jewish Way in Death and Mourning,* just in case. A friend's handwritten inscription stopped me: "To B.J. and Julian, Live long and well—and know only fruitful times. They do come." Suddenly I was not on the way to see my father, possibly for the last time, but at my daughter Ruth's burial 20 years earlier, Dad at my side, supporting me as friends and family shoveled dirt into the open grave a week before her 14th birthday.

I shook my head to clear it. I would not let myself sink into the unbearable. Despite an underlying pain, fruitful days had returned. But now I was facing my father's death, not tragic but certainly not welcome. I leaned forward as if to make the plane go faster. What if Dad died before I got to Atlanta? What if I didn't have a chance for one final visit, to tell him again how much I loved and admired him? Why was this plane just hanging in the air?

Martha, Dad's wife, had called the night before. "You'd better get down here. Your father's hemorrhaging rectally, and we're waiting for the ambulance."

After she had given me a few more details, we had ended the conversation with my urgent plea. "Please tell him not to do anything rash—like die—before I get there."

I had made this trip from Rochester to Atlanta every four to six weeks for most of the past year, alternating with my sister Margaret. It seemed that my visits had consistently coincided with hospitalizations, and that I was always the one to help bring him home from the hospital. Would he return home this time, or was this truly the end?

By the time I arrived at his hospital room shortly before noon that March Friday in 2001, Dad had made good-bye calls to friends, spoken to his seven grandchildren, and reminisced with Martha. As strong-willed and lucid at 92 as he'd been at 52, he had made his decision: no probes, no tests, no treatment. He didn't care why he was hemorrhaging. He had lived a full life and was ready to go—before he became a burden to Martha or his daughters.

I leaned over his bed to give him a tearful hug. "Don't forget your promise."

His deep, brown eyes caressed me. "You know I don't believe in an afterlife. But if I *do* see Ruth, I'll give her a hug for you and tell her how much you, and all of us, have missed her."

I wiped my eyes, and we did what we always did. We recited our repertoire of silly poetry, including our favorite:

The monkey is a friend of mine,
In fact I've heard it stated,
That he and me and me and he
Are distantly related...

I made a mental note to teach it to my grandchildren someday, perhaps to Joey, now barely five months old, named for his great-granddad Joe.

Martha later told me that during that long night, Dad had said to her, "This Joe's dying, and there's another little Joe to go on living." I silently blessed my son and his wife for naming their baby for his living grandfather, even though most northern European Jews name their children for loved ones who have already died.

By the time Margaret arrived, we were on to politics and the economy. Periodically Dad hemorrhaged and complained about being "nothing but a pile of shit," unusual language for him. Margaret or I would call the nurse to clean him up, then we'd resume our conversation. I couldn't bear the thought that these were my last hours with my lifetime hero, but I took my cue from him and focused on the moment.

B.J., Dad, and Margaret

Time passed slowly...and too quickly. The hospital was not pleased that someone refusing treatment was taking up a bed. Margaret and I sought information about hospice placement.

As the day dragged on and Dad rested quietly, my thoughts turned to Shabbat, the Sabbath, which would begin in a few hours, at sundown. I had packed a pair of candles in my suitcase the previous evening. Would I be allowed to light them at the hospital? Probably not. And what about food? I didn't drive, shop, or cook on Shabbat, but somehow I'd manage. I would surely find a can of tuna on Dad's pantry shelves, and the brand he usually bought was kosher.

"I want one of you girls to take Martha home so she can get some rest," said Dad, still in command.

"Yes, a long bath would revive me." Martha had accompanied Dad in the ambulance the evening before and hadn't washed or slept since.

"B.J., why don't you go so you can see if there's anything in the house you can eat," suggested Margaret, always considerate of my more traditional religious practices.

Loath to leave Dad's bedside, I agreed reluctantly. "I guess I should check."

Dad, now as pale as the hospital sheets, turned to me. His voice was steadier than my tearful one, his question typically straightforward and pointed: "Will you come back, even if it's already dark and your Shabbat has begun?"

Dad and I had always been close, but I had strayed in one respect. He believed that being an ethical, upright person made him a good Jew. I agreed that it made him a good person—in fact, I considered him an outstanding one! But I had grown to believe that to be a good Jew included observing the Sabbath, the dietary laws, and other ritual commandments in addition to those that govern relationships between people. This was going to be tricky.

Remember the Sabbath day to keep it holy, or Honor your father and your mother? Two commandments; one chance to get it right. Shabbat was a day on which I didn't travel by automobile, didn't turn on a stove, didn't flick lights on and off—and, perhaps because of those and other restrictions, it was a day that brought peace and balance to my life. My observance of Shabbat strengthened my ties to Judaism and especially to my community. But here was my father, whom I had admired throughout my life for his integrity and love, his loyalty to my mother during her long illness, and his compassionate guidance when I faced my toughest challenges. "Remember you have two other children," he had gently chided me in a letter a few months after Ruth's death. "You can't go back; you must go forward, for their sake, if not your own."

Without hesitation, I spoke through my tears. "Y'know, Dad, there's commandment number four and there's number five. Next week I'll be able to keep Shabbat, but I won't be able to honor you. I'll be back."

Smiling, Dad turned his face up to accept my kiss. I picked up my suitcase and led Martha from the room.

Martha settled into the taxi with a deep sigh and no apparent desire to talk. As the driver maneuvered down Peachtree Road, I watched for the familiar landmarks that always made me feel I was home. A few storefronts and apartment buildings looked as I remembered them, surprising considering Atlanta's boom since I had grown up here in the 1940s and '50s. Despite new facades and additions, I recognized the Catholic, Baptist, Episcopal, and Presbyterian churches, and finally the Methodist one where my Girl Scout troop had met. Just a mile before we turned off Peachtree to my childhood home, I shuddered as I always did at the concrete and glass hotel on the former site of my grandparents' bungalow. Even after all these years, I missed the crazy little cottage set amid evidence of Granddad's green thumb: five acres of jonquils, fig trees, my favorite climbing tree, strawberries, and the scuppernong grape arbor under which I had read on summer afternoons.

The changes to even the familiar landmarks reminded me that Atlanta was no longer the same, and, despite my rich and joyful memories, neither was I.

2

Passover in 1945, as with all seders at my grandparents' bungalow, brings my family—including aunts, uncles, and cousins—together around a table elaborately set with gold-banded plates and crystal goblets. Granddad conducts the short service in English, punctuated by blessings in Hebrew read from the English transliteration. As we go around the table, we younger ones show off our reading skills. As children, we don't always understand the causes of the laughter, but we love the evening's festive gaiety. I especially love searching for the afikomen, a hidden piece of matzah that must be redeemed and eaten before the ritual meal can end. My white-mustached, mostly bald grandfather gives us a clue. "It's behind Elinor," he says repeatedly. I trail my 10-year-older cousin, wondering how it could possibly be behind her when she keeps moving and I am behind her.

"Here it is!" shouts another cousin, triumphantly removing it from behind Elinor's picture on the bookcase.

The food is abundant, starting with the parsley we dip in salt water, matzah, yukky bitter herbs, my mother's marble-sized matzo balls, roast lamb, and ending with my aunt's steamed prune pudding. I can still hear the drama with which we recite "Dayenu" and "It came to pass at midnight." Racing to be the first to finish each verse of "Who Knows One?" and chanting, "An only kid, an only kid" in singsong unison carry us to a rousing finish.

At the seder's conclusion, while the maid clears and washes the dishes, we adjourn to the living room to play "The Game." Don't all seders include charades?

* * *

Hanukkah was a more intimate celebration, just our immediate family. I can still picture us at dinner when I am 9 or so. Mom sits at the head of the table, Dad on the side, so that when they finish eating they can hold hands. We three girls take the remaining seats. Wrapped gifts are at our places, a green and red holly arrangement at the table's center, a silver menorah beside it. Mom lights the *shammash,* then uses this candle to light the others. She recites the blessing in English.

Then Daddy takes over with his own tradition. Playfully, we name each of the candles—perhaps five this night—for a member of the Temple and bet on which will burn the longest: Rabbi Rothschild, the executive director, our Sunday School teachers, Robert (the janitor). After dinner, we linger at the table to see which slim orange candle will win.

Hanukkah and Passover weren't the only times we were festive. My mother loved to celebrate and seized any excuse to decorate and give gifts. While the Hanukkah candles glowed in the dining room, a Christmas tree lit up the living room. My sisters and I anticipated eight Hanukkah gifts, one a night, as well as Christmas presents from our parents and Santa Claus. What kid wouldn't find this abundance irresistible? We also loved hanging colorful balls on the tree, arranging the lights just so, adding shimmering icicles. The place of honor on top? Perhaps a Santa Claus or some mistletoe. Definitely not a star or an angel. Mom drew the line at these religious symbols.

Mother also orchestrated an Easter celebration. How could she let the day pass without our own egg hunt? She helped us dye eggs, and on Easter morning she hid them. With giggling delight, we found them under the couch, on the mantel, inside a newspaper. Afterwards, we picked through shredded cellophane to find the candy "the Easter bunny" had tucked inside colorful baskets.

Despite my mother's love of the Christian celebrations that permeated our Atlanta landscape, we were Jews. Not assimilated. Not indifferent. Jewish.

We belonged to Atlanta's Hebrew Benevolent Congregation, generally known as the Temple. The majestic building sat on a hill overlooking Peachtree Road. A golden ark dominated the sanctuary. When it was time for the Torah reading, the gold door magically lowered to reveal the Torah scrolls within. When the rabbi had returned the scroll to its resting place, the door rose by itself, just as mysteriously from the viewpoint of a child too small to see the electrical switch.

When Daddy was on the board, as he often was, we attended Friday night services. That we attended services on the Jewish New Year and Yom Kippur, the Day of Atonement, went without saying. When I was ten, I fasted on Yom Kippur for the first time. I spent that afternoon at a Jewish friend's house and felt virtuous and a bit smug when I refused the snacks her mother offered. But Sabbath services and minimal holiday celebrations were the extent of our religious practice. I was dimly aware that there were some Jews who didn't eat ham or bacon, but I didn't know any.

My sisters and I went to Sunday school for two hours every week from kindergarten on. I learned the usual Bible stories from creation through the Ten Commandments. Then we skipped right over Leviticus and other books filled with 'thou shall…' and 'thou shalt not…' to the more action-packed tales of Joshua at Jericho, Ruth and Naomi, and on to the prophets. Most of my Sunday School memories, however, are less about content and more about our clothes—poodle skirts—and the titles of the textbooks. *When the Jewish People Was Young* and *How the Jewish People Lives Today* created a stir in my house because of the grammatical implications of "peoplehood" versus individual Jews.

To the limited extent that my family thought about the Bible, we viewed it less as the revealed bedrock of Jewish law and lore than as an inspired book pointing the way to social justice.

My parents' pursuit of justice dominated dinnertime conversations. Although Dad sometimes engaged us in math and geography games (I still know state capitals by Daddy's silly clues), more often my parents talked about local politics and their own civic activities. Struggling to solve a math problem in my head was a joy compared to hearing about the corruption and bigotry that colored Georgia politics. Mother, who had grown up in Seattle, was more liberal than her Atlanta-born husband, but Dad worked hard to help Atlanta fulfill its 1950s motto, "A City Too Busy To Hate." At one point, he chaired the Community Chest campaign. For a year or two he was president of Atlanta Family Service Society. He droned through dinner about these and other issues and involvements. Mother gave her time to the National Council of Jewish Women and the League of Women Voters. She and her friends started a project that helped "old folks" (even older than they were) find jobs. I remember Dad's interest in her lengthy tales of serving on a jury. But for me, it was all boring, boring, boring. I couldn't wait to run outside to play catch with Dad and my older sister, Leslie. Margaret, 6 years my junior, was too young to join us.

1946: Mom, Leslie, Margaret, Dad, and B.J.

Throughout most of my childhood, I never thought much about being Jewish. As far as I could tell, the only difference between me and my school friends was that they went to church and I went to Temple. Until December, that is: Christmas permeated my public school, my Scout troop, all facets of my life. I particularly remember the uneasy discomfort when my class sang carols.

God rest you merry, gentlemen
Let nothing you dismay
Remember HUM HUM HU-U-UM
Was born on Christmas Day.

But it wasn't always easy to hum my way around the issue of religion. When I was in fourth grade, the unthinkable happened. My best friend, Eloise Danielle Wilson, Danny for short, called one night to say she couldn't play with me anymore. I stood in the downstairs hall, holding the black receiver to my ear, trying to understand.

"Why?" I asked, voice trembling. "Did I do something bad?"

Her voice was quiet, uncertain. "Because my parents said so." We were both good girls, who did what we were told.

How could this be? My best friend. We played at each other's houses, did homework together, whispered together at lunchtime, tried to be on the same team at recess. All that was now gone? For no good reason?

With lowered head, I shuffled into the living room. Daddy sat at a card table, writing checks. Mom sat across from him, addressing envelopes for the paid bills. They looked up as I came in.

"Danny says we can't be friends any more." I couldn't hold back my tears. "She says she can't come over here to play. Her parents won't let her."

Mom hugged me. "Don't worry, dear. I know you're disappointed, but I know you. Before long you'll have another best friend."

Daddy patted me on the shoulder. As I turned to go upstairs and sulk in my bedroom, I heard him mumble something about being Jewish. Was *that* why Danny's parents ended our friendship? Because we were Jewish?

And how did Daddy know? Had he or Mommy experienced something similar? Although their inner circle comprised Temple members, they counted a fair number of Christians among their friends. They seemed well-respected and liked by everyone.

At this first personal experience of anti-Semitism, I was hurt and confused. I remembered hearing about the singsong playground taunts my sister had endured when she was in second grade: "Leslie doesn't believe in Jesus, Leslie doesn't believe in Jesus." But whereas Les was always a little out of step socially, I fit in with my classmates. At least I thought I did. Apparently, that wasn't enough.

Leslie, Margaret, and B.J.

When Leslie and I fought—or got in trouble together—I quickly learned to apologize and then keep quiet. While her loud self-justifications brought all the negative attention to herself, I slipped out of the room. It didn't win points with my sister, but it taught me a valuable lesson about accepting blame and moving on. The situation with Danny was different, however. What was I responsible for? All I could do was swallow my distress and seek new playmates.

Two years after my friendship with Danny ended, I stood every morning with the other students in Mrs. Bowden's sixth grade class to recite the Lord's Prayer and Pledge of Allegiance. We sat while Mrs. Bowden continued, as did all teachers in Atlanta public schools in the 1940s and '50s, with a devotional reading. I didn't know which annoyed me more, her devotionals about Jesus or her constant bragging about being Senator Russell's sister.

One morning—a morning that still haunts me—she read a selection from her New Testament, then directed, "Would whoever doesn't believe in Jesus please stand up."

How dare she single me out in front of my friends? Fury mingled with embarrassment as one other girl and I, faces red, knees wobbly, stumbled to our feet.

"And who is your great leader?" Despite her southern drawl, her words stung.

Mortified beyond thought, I had no answer. "Um, er, ah ….," was the best I could manage.

"Moses," she answered for us. I wish now that I'd had the presence of mind to say "God."

When I told my parents, they were as upset as I. The next morning, I walked up to Mrs. Bowden and held out a Sunday School book, *When the Jewish People Was Young*. Mom had prompted me what to say.

"Mrs. Bowden, since you seem so interested in my religion, maybe you'd like to read this book."

I don't remember any verbal response, but without a smile, she accepted the offering and placed it on her desk.

I was proud of being Jewish, and I didn't understand why my teacher should embarrass me for that. Although I still missed my closeness with Danny, I had a new best friend. I played with her and other classmates after school. Most of the time I didn't feel any different from the other kids in my class. And yet, there was the annual Sunday that the Methodist minister invited the members of all the Girl Scout troops that met at his church to worship with his congregation. I went with my friends, but all that Jesus stuff made me uncomfortable. I was beginning to get the message that despite Christmas trees and Easter egg hunts, I was an outsider.

3

As if an invisible fence had been erected, many of the girls with whom I had played after school, at their homes or mine, stopped asking me over once we moved to the high school building in eighth grade. The one non-Jewish friend who invited me anywhere was Bill, who took me on his Presbyterian Church hayrides. He tried to convert me, and I responded in kind, both of us knowing that we were too committed to our own faiths to take the other's arguments seriously.

Had we lived in a different neighborhood, I might have attended Grady High School, where about a third of the students were Jewish. But at white Anglo-Saxon Protestant North Fulton High, where the Student Christian Fellowship was the dominant student club, I was one of half a dozen Jewish kids in the class of 1957.

Religious school and the Temple's youth group became the focus of my social life. From eighth grade on, I attended Religious school on Saturday mornings. Then we went to services, where I sat with my class. Nana, my dad's mother, had gone to temple every Sabbath morning. Starting at about the time she died, I did the same. I liked becoming familiar with the prayers. I liked the enforced quiet time. Most of my friends grumbled about spending Saturday mornings cooped up. They could hardly wait for services to end. Together, we would traverse Peachtree Road for hamburgers and fried onions at Crossroads, followed by a bus ride downtown to window shop. I enjoyed Saturday afternoons with my friends, but unlike them, and although I didn't admit it, I also found services satisfying in some indefinable way.

My tenth grade religious school teacher urged her students to welcome the Sabbath by lighting candles and reciting the blessing over the wine. This was the first time I had heard of a Reform Jew lighting Sabbath candles. I was both surprised and intrigued. Ever the dutiful student, I broached the idea to Mom. My mild-mannered mother was furious. "How dare your teacher tell us what we should do in our own home!" The idea fizzled, a candle in a cloudburst. The suggestion took root in my mind, however, a tender shoot thirsty for more.

One boy in my religious school class, Eddie, had a bar mitzvah—at the Conservative synagogue. I wondered why, though I never asked. Reform Jews of that era, or at least in our congregation, did not celebrate the traditional coming of age at 13. (The Conservative movement was just beginning to offer the parallel service, bat mitzvah, to girls in the 1950s.) Apparently, our rabbi feared that students would drop out after the bar mitzvah, during seventh or eighth grade. Instead, we all (including Eddie) continued through the tenth grade for confirmation, a group ceremony that we took seriously as affirming our commitment to Judaism. We selected for our motto a line from the prophet Micah (6:8): "It has been told you, O man, what is good, and what the Lord requires of you: only to do justly, and to love mercy, and to walk humbly with your God."

Looking back, I see how many elements of the holiday of Shavuot, which commemorates the biblical account of Moses receiving the Ten Commandments at Mount Sinai, were woven into our 1955 confirmation ceremony.

I knew nothing of sacrifices and offerings in the ancient Temple of yore, but was elated to be selected to give the "floral prayer," considered the plum part. My parents helped me practice the prayer I had been given.

"Slow down," Dad said, each time I began.

"Louder," Mom reminded me.

Slowly, too loudly for our living room, I recited from memory the prayer that ended with these words from Isaiah: "The grass withereth, the flower fadeth, but the word of the Lord endureth forever."

"Be careful," Dad said just before that line.

And even so, I slipped and ended, "but the word of the Lord endureth forevereth."

We all laughed, Dad reminded me to go slowly, Mom warned me to be careful, and I would go through it again, usually concluding with "forevereth."

I'm sure my parents held their breaths that Sunday morning in May 1955 as we girls, dressed in white robes accented by bouquets of deep red roses, climbed the curved stairs in our high-heeled shoes to place our floral offerings in the ark in front of the Torah scrolls. To my family's relief, I completed my part without the extra "eth."

A reception, a party, copious gifts, an equal number of thank-you notes, and my religious school days ended. But it seems that the enduring word of God lingered in my soul… forevereth.

After confirmation, I continued to be active in Temple Youth Group during my last two years of high school. Attending bi-weekly discussions led by our rabbi for post-confirmation teens, participating in regular youth group meetings and projects, and occasionally going to services with my family, I was, in my estimation, a good Jew.

One summer, I spent two weeks at the national youth group conclave. I was astonished that one of the boys, a teenager like me, knew enough Hebrew to read from the Torah scroll. When the congregation of kids, all of them around my own age, sang the Aleynu prayer, I listened, mouth agape. The others knew this prayer in Hebrew, a subject that simply wasn't taught at the Temple. Yet these kids were also Reform. Was I the only person at this Reform Leadership Institute who hadn't been taught the language? I knew (by rote) precisely two Hebrew prayers: the six-word Sh'ma and Ayn K'Eloheinu, a repetitious paean to God. And I could read them only in transliteration. I did not know how to read the Hebrew characters—the only way I could read Hebrew was if it was written out in English letters!

When Institute counselors taught Hebrew songs, I was limited not only by my inability to carry a tune but also by my unfamiliarity with Hebrew words and phrases. Tucking away the wistful feeling that others, who were my age and probably no smarter, knew at least some Hebrew, I settled into the Institute's rhythm of discussion groups and leadership seminars. We sat outdoors on the green lawn to explore why we as Jews should care about injustice and to consider how we could work to make our world a more caring and just place to live. This was the Judaism that I knew and felt comfortable with. This was what I had absorbed from my family background, knowledge, and experience: how to "do justly, love mercy, and walk humbly with God." These were ideas I could bring home to my youth group. My lack of Hebrew skills didn't matter here, and the inadequacy I had felt soon vanished.

Back in Atlanta, our youth group met every Sunday night for a brief program followed by dancing, which was the main attraction, especially since Georgia Tech's Jewish students often showed up. One year, I was in charge of giving the opening prayer; another, I was project chair. During my junior year in high school, the Bureau of Jewish Education planned a program to bring all of Atlanta's Jewish teens together. I was asked to be the Temple Youth Group representative on a panel discussion that would precede the social gathering. The president of the Conservative youth group drove from Grady High to North Fulton in his blue and white '55 Chevy Bel Air to take me to the planning meeting. I remember the scenario going something like this:

I opened the passenger door cautiously. "Julian?"

"Hey, B.J." A scrawny, kinda-cute guy turned down the radio, and I climbed in. He started the car and asked, "What grade are you in?"

"I'm a junior. How about you?"

"A senior."

"Oh."

"Do you know Liz Jacobson?" he asked.

"Sure, she's my best friend. How do you know her?"

"I've met her at dances."

"Oh."

Though I have little recollection of the car ride or planning the meeting with the boy who would later become such a vital part of my life, a single, lined 3"x 5" card titled "Jewish Youth & The Synagogue" has somehow survived. Here are my hand-printed notes for my share of the panel discussion:

Religious school and services—not enough.

Need for furthering religious education—just when interest develops, s. school stops.

Need filled through Youth Group—group discussions, participation in services—

Become interested in helping Y.G.—later this interest turns to community—important as Jews to take part in community activities.

Community won't come to us—we must go to it!

At the event itself, my new friend Julian invited me to dance.

"Would you buy a ticket to 'Doctor at Sea'?" I asked as we jitterbugged. "Youth Group is selling tickets for a fundraiser, and I'm project chairman."

"I'll buy two if you'll go with me." His Chattahoochee River-brown eyes smiled through his glasses as he spun me away from him and caught my outstretched hand before I twirled out of reach.

I already had plans to see the movie, but I needed to sell tickets. And besides, he was a good dancer and seemed smart. "Sure, I'd love to."

By the time the music stopped, we had planned our first date. I had no inkling that this was the beginning of a lifelong friendship and romance.

My sense of being an outsider at school intensified when North Fulton High's student body vice president lined up students to give the daily devotional over the public address system. During my senior year, a school friend since first grade did the honors. Perhaps with thoughts of social action gleaned from my youth group summer Leadership Institute in mind, I approached her about the devotional contents.

"Wyn," I asked her, "would you please remind people that not everyone in this school believes in Jesus. When they end their prayers 'in Jesus' name, amen,' I can't not hear those words. But if they left them off, anyone who wanted could say them in their heads."

"I'll try," she said.

Before long, my friend Bill and others complained to me. "A prayer isn't complete if it's not in Jesus' name," Bill insisted.

"But you can add it for yourself," I argued. "I can't block out words coming over the loud speaker, even if I don't believe or accept them. It just cancels out the whole prayer for me."

And on we argued, good-naturedly but seriously.

As graduation approached, I was still out of step with the majority of my classmates, though I represented them all as class valedictorian. Fortunately, I had the security of a close circle of Jewish friends and a loving family from whom I had absorbed social justice, community involvement, and intellectual curiosity. I was ready to head out into the world.

4

How is this night different from all other nights? On all other seder nights, I have celebrated the Exodus from Egypt. But on this Passover night in 1959, I sit at my desk in my college dorm room plowing through a reading assignment. Strains of music drift through my slightly open window. Looking up, I see a group of students walking arm in arm across the well-lit Smith College campus. Their voices ring out with a lusty rendition of a favorite seder song: "Di-di-aynu, di-di-aynu." Judging by the girls' laughter, I had missed a spirited evening.

The melody tears at my heart, and I sigh with regret. Why did I choose to stay behind? I've never missed a seder before. Last year I attended the festive Passover meal that Hillel Foundation sponsors annually for Smith and neighboring colleges. But this year I succumbed to a daunting workload. I chastise myself for denying myself the connections to my childhood seders and my faith. Too late now, I think. With another sigh, I turn back to the textbook. I have no way to know that in twenty years or so I will again feel disconsolate on a seder night—not just an unhappy pang from my own poor choice but with a grief far more profound than I could imagine in my youth.

* * *

Almost two years earlier, in the fall of 1957, I had nervously boarded a train in Atlanta for Northampton, Massachusetts. We had already shipped my clothing in the wardrobe trunk that my Aunt Jo had used at Smith a generation earlier. The upperclassmen who met me at the station allayed my apprehensions with their warm welcome. As I got to know the girls (that's what we called ourselves), I discovered that all Jewish freshman were assigned Jewish roommates. Did that mean that others wouldn't want to room with us? Or that most Jews were more comfortable with each other than with "the other"? I didn't dwell on the conundrum but settled comfortably into college life, making friends based on common interests rather than religion. My Jewish roommate and I got along okay, but I wasn't sorry when she chose to move to a different dorm the next year.

One October 1958 morning, early in my sophomore year, a friend approached me.

"B.J., did you hear about the bombing in Atlanta?"

I was instantly alert. "What bombing? Who? Where?"

"A temple."

"Temple? Oh no!" The Temple, my temple, was the only Atlanta synagogue consistently referred to that way. The news exploded inside me. I pictured books I had prayed from in tattered heaps, imagined the Ark surrounded by rubble. I dashed to the payphone to call my parents, uncontrollable trembling making it difficult to dial. In a voice tinged with anger and sorrow, Mother filled me in. Robert, the custodian who had cared for the Temple throughout my childhood, had discovered the pre-dawn explosion when he arrived to open the building at 7:15. A few hours later, it would have been filled with Religious school students and teachers. Just the thought of what might have been intensified my shaking. I felt too ill to study and spent the day in bed.

The greatest damage was to the Temple's exterior wall, I saw a few days later when I pored over the newspaper clippings Mom sent me. Bricks, twisted pipes, and fallen plaster filled familiar offices and hallways. By some miracle, the sanctuary, including the gas-fueled eternal light, was unharmed, although shards of stained glass littered the floor.

Mother's letter accompanying the article and photographs indicated that the perpetrators were assumed to be militant white supremacists expressing their resistance to integration and the civil rights movement. (Five men were later tried and acquitted.) She reminded me of the numerous sermons that Pittsburgh-born Rabbi Rothschild had given on the subject. While distraught over the bombing, she was pleased that her rabbi was a leader in interfaith and interracial dialogue. Four years earlier, he had drafted the Atlanta clergy's response to the 1954 Supreme Court decision ending the South's "separate but equal" justification of segregated schools. With this encouragement, the Atlanta school board had produced an integration plan that was painfully slow but, unlike the ones in Montgomery, Alabama, and Little Rock, Arkansas, had proceeded without violence.

No doubt the white radical groups had hoped the blast would ignite a full-scale race war against Jews and blacks in Atlanta. Instead, I learned from the newspaper and Mom's subsequent letters, it broke through the moderates' wall of silence. Mayor Hartsfield had arrived at the Temple within minutes of hearing the news. "It is high time that decent people of the South rise and take charge if governmental chaos is to be avoided," he declared. Editor Ralph McGill put it this way in *The Atlanta Constitution*:

"Dynamite in great quantity ripped a beautiful temple of worship in Atlanta.... It is the crop of things sown. It is the harvest of defiance of the courts...the harvest of those who have chosen to preach hate instead of compassion... You do not preach and encourage hatred for the Negro and hope to restrict it to that field."

I thought back to my confirmation class motto: "What does God require of you? Only to do justice, to love mercy, and to walk humbly with God." Like my parents, I was proud that our rabbi stood up for justice, even though in the next months my whole body shivered whenever thoughts of the bombing surfaced.

But Judaism made little difference to my daily college life. I attended services on the High Holidays, but rarely on the Sabbath. My primary religious involvement was academic, intellectual. Freshman year I took a course in "Bible as Literature," and although it was taught by one of the world's most boring professors, I found it intriguing. Sophomore year, I took a religion course that involved reading Catholic, Protestant, and Jewish theologians. No matter how fascinating the arguments of the Christian thinkers, the words of the Jewish writers resonated with something inside me. Each time I got to Martin Buber, the Jewish theologian most often assigned, I sighed with the comfort of coming home.

At the time, I didn't understand how far he was out of the Jewish mainstream. But his writing about a God with whom we relate in intimate dialogue confirmed my own spiritual sensibility. Buber's ideas enlarged my understanding of covenant from abstraction to a living relationship between a God who acts in history and His people. I especially liked Buber's concept that God's covenantal promise to give Abraham's descendants the land had created the "soul" of Israel, while His revelation at Sinai established the people Israel's "body." I'm no longer sure which of Buber's writings I studied that year and which later, but in that class, I clarified two things about myself: I enjoyed the intellectual challenge of reading theology so much that I decided to major in religion, and, despite my fascination with world religions, I was emotionally grounded in Judaism.

My interest in Judaism was more theological than practical. In a later seminar on Judaism, I learned that Orthodox Jews believe that God revealed both the written law (Torah, Pentateuch) and the oral law (rabbinic interpretation as recorded in the Talmud) to Moses at Mount Sinai. That's why, I realized, Orthodox Jews clung to the past and observed all those laws and rituals that we Reform Jews had cast off a century ago. Like most Reform Jews of that era, I believed that the Torah was written by divinely inspired humans. If rabbis of earlier generations chose to spend their lives interpreting it, their interpretations applied to their time, not mine.

"Sachar brushes over theology and philosophy; he is purely a historian—*malheureusement!*" reads a note I penciled in the margin of the Jewish history book that was our course text. The Jewish history I learned that semester was interesting, but I felt no more personal connection with the Jews of talmudic or medieval times than I did with the Hindus or Buddhists, whose writings also intrigued me. My story was that of southern, Reform, American Jewry—and prophetic Judaism.

I loved studying the prophets, especially Amos and Jeremiah. Unlike the Talmudic rabbis (about whom I knew virtually nothing), the prophets seemed like real people, men with personalities, goals, disappointments, and individual relationships with God. Jeremiah seemed so lonely and anguished as he warned the people of their impending exile, and yet full of promise when he told them that God would write His covenant upon their hearts, forever. Amos's explanation of the Jews' chosenness made sense to me: "You, only, have I [God] known of all the families of the earth; therefore will I punish you for all your iniquities." (Amos 3:2). Because of the special relationship with the people Israel, God places greater requirements on them. And how to meet those demands? Sacrifices and burnt offerings will not please the Lord, says

Amos, "but let justice roll down like waters, and righteousness like an ever-flowing stream." (5:24) *This* was my religion.

Jewish study supported the beliefs I had absorbed growing up: beliefs in how to relate to God, how to fulfill God's expectations of kindness and justice. When an Atlanta friend asked me, at a party during Christmas vacation, what I would do with a religion major, I answered, somewhat smugly, "Live."

5

Spring of my sophomore year, Dad came to Northampton for father's weekend. I was thrilled to have a few days alone with my favorite man. I showed him around the campus and proudly introduced him to my friends. Dad and I had always had a special relationship. He set high standards, and, with the exception of carrying a tune, I generally met them. Moreover, I laughed at his jokes, groaned at his puns, and just enjoyed being with him. That weekend, when we lost a tennis match to a friend and her dad, my competitive father (who had invested heavily in tennis lessons for me) and I consoled ourselves that we had never before played as partners, never admitting that they were better than we were.

As we sat in my dorm lobby that evening waiting for dinner, Dad mused aloud. "My parents lived modestly, but they were able to send their four children to college and two of us to graduate school. Following in their footsteps, I've sent Leslie to Oberlin, you to Smith, and hopefully Margaret will go wherever she chooses when the time comes."

I listened attentively.

Dad continued. "I believe a father owes his children three things: love, an education, and a good heritage. Any financial gift is a bonus."

I hugged him. "That makes sense. You've certainly given me the foundation for a good life. I didn't understand until I heard Smith friends talk about their families just how lucky I am. And I love Smith. Thank you."

Mother and Dad had surely given me love and the best education. I never asked what he meant by "good heritage," but in later years I came to equate it with Jewish values: a high moral standard, loyalty to one's family, an urge for community service, and a continuous quest to learn. Forty plus years later, as he lay dying, I would recall his words, which were, essentially, an ethical will. Even when I was 20, I knew that he had blessed me with great wisdom. Lucky, lucky me.

6

I spent the summer after my sophomore year living with a family in France, then traveling with a group of American and French young people, all participants in the Experiment in International Living. My host family, the Soubeyrans, had three young children but no teenager. The family lived in Ecully, a village a few kilometers west of Lyon. I enjoyed their simple lifestyle. I spent my days reading in the garden, helping Mme. Soubeyran market, and exploring my surroundings. When the Experiment leaders planned group sightseeing or social events, I joined them.

In the evenings, as we exchanged stories, always *en Français,* the Soubeyrans heard stilted anecdotes about Julian, who was now, three years after our first date, my boyfriend. I heard about M. Soubeyran's work at a Lyon café and his wife's tales of her father. During World War II, he had been a railroad conductor on a train that traveled between German-controlled and free France. He delivered messages, hiding them beneath a huge cape, and—if I understood Madame's French correctly—he sometimes helped Jews escape. She was proud that her Papa had played even a small role in the Resistance. I was intrigued. This was the closest I had ever come to a firsthand account of those years—war, resistance, Holocaust.

One evening, their five-year-old, who spoke French at native speed, asked, "Do you dream in French or in English?"

For once I understood. "*Ça depend.* If I dream about France, I dream in French. If I dream about home, I dream in English."

"Then you dream in English," interjected M. Soubeyran with a twinkle in his eye, "because *toujours* you dream of Julian."

One Friday, I rode my *bicyclette* into Lyon. I left it at the apartment where my friend Barb's host family lived and set out with her to sightsee and shop. Late that afternoon, on a whim, I inquired at the city information desk, *"Où est une synagogue Juive?"* and listened intently to the French instructions.

I assured Barb that I could find my way back to her apartment, where I would spend the night prior to a group bicycle trip to a medieval town the next morning. Alone, I set off to find the synagogue and inquire when there were services.

While standing in the courtyard to get my bearings, I heard singing. "Oh yes," I thought. "I've heard of sundown services." I worried that I would never go to Temple in clothing as casual as a peasant skirt, sleeveless blouse, and sandals. But, I reassured myself, I'm a tourist, this is what I'm wearing, and this might be my only chance to visit a synagogue during my summer in France.

I followed the music to the sanctuary and quietly joined the worshipping congregation. A murmur seemed to go through the crowd. Heads turned. People stared. Was it so obvious that I was a stranger? Looking around, I saw that all the women were wearing hats, and my head was bare. "Well, can't help it," I thought, not knowing that because I was an unmarried woman, my head need not be covered. Still, so many eyes, all directed at me. I remembered that one shouldn't carry money on the Sabbath, but who was to know that my wallet was empty. More stares.

I searched the room for a reason. Slowly, finally, I figured it out.

I was standing with the men.

Oh, how I wished I could make myself invisible. As I hurried to the women's side, the congregation seemed to let out its collective breath. A woman graciously made room for me. When I had recovered enough from my embarrassment to listen, I realized that I didn't understand a word. The service was in Hebrew.

"*Est-ce qu'il y a un service en Français*?" I whispered.

"*Oui*, tomorrow."

My embarrassment merited only a few lines in the journal I kept that summer, but I never forgot my bewilderment at that service. After all, I was no stranger to Sabbath services, and I had been the star religious school student. Moreover, I had just declared my religion major in college. Although it didn't necessarily show on the outside, I identified strongly as a Jew. I cared enough to seek out a synagogue on the one Friday that the opportunity arose.

But this experience pointed out to me how little I knew of traditional practices—not only did I not know one letter of Hebrew, I didn't have enough awareness to notice that men and women were seated separately. I was an outsider among my own people.

I wonder if that disastrous visit to a French synagogue influenced the topic of my senior honors thesis: "And You Shall Be My People: A Study of the Jewish Community." Did I, subconsciously perhaps, seek a sense of community through my academic work? Or was my topic designed merely to integrate my fascination with Martin Buber's writings with my love of the prophets?

The thesis started with Buber's understanding of covenant and Zionism, the millennia-old yearning of the Jewish people to return from the Diaspora to Palestine (now Israel). Buber explained that an eternal bond between people and land was created by God's promise to Abraham that "to your descendants I give this land..." (Genesis 15:17). My second chapter revealed Jeremiah helping the Jewish people prepare for life in exile following the destruction of the first Temple by the Babylonians. Without the Temple, sacrificial offerings would be impossible, but Jeremiah insisted that the people could maintain their relationship with God through righteous actions. The third chapter described rabbinic efforts to build a portable community that would withstand the trials of exile after the Roman destruction of the second Temple in 70 C.E. Study of the Torah would provide the societal structure in Diaspora. I concluded that a community that revolved around God, Torah study, justice, and a close bond with the land was the best defense against the materialism and spiritual vacuum that dominated the early 1960s landscape.

While writing passionately about Zionism, I never dreamed I would someday set foot on the land. It never occurred to me that when the rabbis touted the importance of study, they were really discussing ritual and ethics—the proper interpretation and performance of biblical statements relating to dietary laws, prayer, Sabbath and holiday observance, just weights and measures, and every other detail of life.

At the time, I considered my thesis an academic exercise, no more a faith statement than my English major friend's thesis on the author Iris Murdoch. My only conscious goal was to complete the honors program requirements. Rereading it 50 years later, I am astonished at its scope and ardor. It took decades for my experiences to catch up with what I apparently "knew" as a college senior.

Although I devoted my senior thesis to a study of Jewish community, I wrote it from the perspective of semi-outsider, not as someone deeply immersed in its daily life. It combined my intellectual fascination with the prophets and Buber, but it didn't enhance my closeness to God or my people. That would come later.

7

"This will be my first-ever second seder," I remind Julian in 1962, during the 15-minute drive from our apartment to his parents' home. "Just think, two nights to celebrate my favorite holiday."

Deciding which night to go to which seder was easy: Following Reform custom, my family observes only one, while Julian's Conservative family celebrates two.

"It will be different, and you won't understand the Hebrew," Julian warns me, "and there may be fewer people than you're used to. My sisters will be with their in-laws for the second night." Three of Julian's four siblings live in Atlanta, along with nine of my 13 newly acquired nieces and nephews.

With a welcoming kiss, Julian's mother bustles us into the living room. I listen happily to the conversation that swirls about me. When the last guest arrives, we move into the dining room. I pick up a slim paperback Haggadah with the Maxwell House Coffee logo on the cover. Leafing through it, I see pages black with Hebrew squiggles that I still can't read. Thank heavens for the English translation.

We fill our glasses with wine, and Julian's dad, at the head of the table, be-

gins rattling off the Hebrew. Huh? This is a seder? Last night, my dad read most of the first prayer, the sanctification of the wine, in English, then we all joined together for the final Hebrew words. His Southern-accented voice was slow and clear, and throughout the evening he gave us each a turn to read. Family jokes developed over many years punctuated the evening with laughter and gaiety. But that was last night. Tonight I have trouble following the hurried service, and from time to time Julian points out the place.

We arrive at the blessing over a spring vegetable—at last, something familiar. But instead of the crisp, curly, green parsley I expect, we dip drab potato slices into the salt water. I suppose this is in deference to the family's Eastern European roots.

A minute or two later we pause while the youngest grandchild asks the four questions. And then my father-in-law continues mumbling unfamiliar sounds until I recognize "Dayenu" and the blessings for matzah and bitter herbs. We pause for a delicious meal. My mother-in-law, a fabulous cook, serves homemade gefilte fish, chicken soup, brisket, and all the trimmings.

"I've never seen such huge matzah balls," I whisper to Julian when the soup is served. They're like tennis balls, so different from the marble-sized ones Mom prides herself in making. I take a bite. "Yum! Fluffy and delicious," I say loudly enough for my mother-in-law to hear.

Later that night, driving home, Julian and I discuss the differences: more Hebrew, a faster pace, less laughter, and food discrepancies. "Do you think it's a reflection of basic distinctions between Reform and Conservative Judaism?" I ask him. "Or evidence that as a rerun, a second seder is less important than the first?"

"Ours may be fast, but it's complete," he says. "Look how much yours omits from the traditional Hagaddah."

"That may be, but at least we love what we do," I retort.

We both hope that next year I'll be more comfortable at my in-laws' seder.

Later that week, we accept Mom's invitation to a small party. I help myself to a brownie from the dining room table. Julian declines.

"No brownie?" I ask in surprise.

"No, they aren't Pesa-stickie."

"Pesa-stickie? What's that?" I ask.

"It means they're not right for Passover," he explains. "I don't eat anything

with leavening or regular flour during the holiday."

For the first time, it dawns on me that eating unleavened bread is intended to be more than a one-night affair. My family has never changed our eating habits for Passover. We've never avoided the grains that Julian now tells me are forbidden during the entire eight-day festival. Why should breakfast (or any meal) during Passover be different from all other days? Matzah at the seder, toast or cereal for breakfast the next morning. And what does the food matter when the seder is so rushed and boring?

* * *

Julian and I married two weeks after my 1961 college graduation. His background was more traditional than mine. Whereas my forebears all arrived from Germany in the mid-19th century, his came as part of the turn-of-the-century Eastern European immigration. My family was Reform; his, Conservative. My parents and grandparents were college-educated. His parents were high school-and-library-educated. In fact, in 1914, when his dad's merchant family moved to Atlanta from Greensboro, Georgia (where, as the town's only Jews, they had maintained the Jewish dietary laws, eating kosher meat imported from Atlanta), my grandfather was the attorney who oversaw their purchase of a dry goods store.

Before we married, Julian handed me a book to read about the Eastern European shtetl so that I'd understand the source of some of his family's customs. I was particularly struck by the way village life revolved around the Sabbath, that the rabbi was the revered head of the community who answered practical questions about daily life, and that women waited on the men. In my home, my mother sat at the head of the table and ladies were always served before men. Not so in Julian's, and now I understood why.

My parents had had six years since I first met Julian to get to know him. He was the friend I had invited to a college dance when my boyfriend-of-the-moment couldn't come. He was the friend I had asked to be my date for parties surrounding the wedding of my older sister, who had paved the way by marrying someone of Eastern European Jewish background. During the summer I was in France, Julian had dropped by my parents' home frequently, helping Mother and Dad with the crossword puzzle and sharing censored versions of my letters to him. They were pleased that he formally asked Dad's permission to marry me. They respected his family and were delighted to welcome him as their son-in-law. That mattered to me; pleasing my parents made me happy, too.

Mother cheerfully planned the wedding in the Temple's chapel to be followed by what she called a cocktail buffet, with platters of shrimp and other catered delicacies.

Julian and I visited Rabbi Rothschild to discuss the ceremony. Looking back, I marvel at my groom's flexibility.

"No yarmulke," said the rabbi. Gentlemen don't wear hats inside. No marriage canopy. "The *chuppah* represents the Tabernacle in the Wilderness, which is already symbolized by our chapel with its sloping walls," the rabbi continued.

"Break a glass?" asked my fiancé.

"Absolutely not!" rebuked the rabbi. "That custom represents rupturing virginity, and we can't introduce something so uncouth into the sanctity of the wedding ceremony." I suspect that he found the more commonly cited reasons for this familiar symbol equally distasteful: to remember the destruction of the Temple in Jerusalem or to drive away evil spirits that might congregate at a happy time.

I didn't know enough, nor was I sufficiently assertive, to dispute the rabbi about the wedding. All the customs the rabbi rejected would have seemed exotic to my family. If Julian's family found the ceremony sterile, they kept their opinions to themselves and welcomed me into their clan.

Newlyweds in Atlanta, we had to choose between his Conservative congregation and my Reform one. That fall on Rosh Hashanah, the day that celebrates the start of the Jewish year and begins the ten-day period of repentance that culminates in Yom Kippur, I regretted having bent to Julian's wishes. Although I knew the theoretical differences, I wasn't prepared for the practical implications.

Julian led me down the aisle of the large sanctuary to the Yudelson family pew. I squeezed in between Julian and his mother. The cantor was chanting a Hebrew prayer, and I didn't know any more Hebrew than I had two years earlier in France. I opened my prayer book, glanced at my mother-in-law's book for the page number, then leafed through to find the place. The only trouble was that I was going backwards in these books that went, like the Hebrew language, from right to left. Finally, I found the place and focused my eyes on the English side. But even these words were unfamiliar. Why am I here? I thought. Where are the prayers that I know by heart? Why do people seem to be mumbling at their own pace, not in unison?

I looked around. The women in surrounding rows were decked out in their finest clothes, gaudy jewels, and mink stoles. Mink stoles in Atlanta, in September? Crazy, I thought. The women at the Temple may have dressed just as ostentatiously, but I knew them, I recognized their faces, they were friends to smile at, not strangers to judge.

"Move over," stage-whispered a male voice in the row ahead to a woman I presumed to be part of his extended family.

"These are our seats."

"Move your fat fanny over. We've been sitting here forever."

This seemed more like a raucous family get-together than the church-like decorum I was used to. The service, with its informality, unfamiliar melodies, and incomprehensible language felt as foreign as if I had mistakenly walked into a Latin Mass. I felt increasingly forlorn. Why, I asked myself, weren't we worshipping with *my* family only a few quiet miles away?

"Well, B.J., did you like our services?" asked my father-in-law as we trooped out together.

I nodded, smiled shakily, and didn't answer. I feared that if I opened my mouth, the sobs that were dammed behind my throat would gush forth. My religion major had armed me with theological insights into world religions but had not given me practical tools to deal with my own.

With Julian at work all day as an assistant buyer at Atlanta's premier department store, I found the days long. I could spend only so much time reading or gabbing with neighbors and friends. A product of my generation, I did not expect to enter the workforce. Instead, always comfortable in the student role, I investigated graduate school at Emory University. There was no Judaic studies program at that time. The Old Testament program was for Ph.D. students, but when I discovered that

I would have to learn not only Hebrew, but Greek, Syriac, Aramaic, Ugaritic, and another ancient Semitic language or two, as well as German, I begged the administration to create a master's program for me. I wanted to study Bible, not become a linguist. They agreed, but because Emory was a Methodist theology school they required me to take two undergraduate courses not included in my religion major, Pauline theology and early church history. In one of those courses I encountered Ruby Beadle.

At least twice and maybe three times my age, Ruby continually challenged the professor with questions and statements that sought to rewrite church history and theology to match her right-wing, fundamentalist agenda. Her constant interruptions distracted and annoyed me and my classmates. One day I mentioned her to Mother.

"So that's where Ruby Beadle went."

"You know Ruby?" I asked.

"She was in my League of Women Voters unit. She's a John Bircher, and she drove us all crazy with her warped view of the Constitution and politics."

"She drives us crazy, too. It seems like she's not there to learn but to spout her opinions."

Mother gave me a sympathetic smile. "I was glad when she left our group, but I never dreamed you'd be stuck with her. I'm so sorry."

One day Ruby approached me after class. "Your beliefs and mine aren't really that far apart," she said.

I stared at her. I couldn't imagine a single political, social, or religious idea that we shared.

"If you'd give me a chance, I could explain both religions so that you'd see that there's really no difference between Christianity and Judaism," she continued. "All you have to do is acknowledge Christ's divinity and the rest falls in place."

"And when you're done explaining, what's left won't be my religion. No, thank you." I walked away, proud of myself for rebutting her overture to convert me. Although I was struggling to adjust to the new rituals I encountered by my "mixed marriage" to a Conservative Jew, I was unequivocally and happily Jewish.

The following summer, I approached the Bureau of Jewish Education and was promised that if I could assemble a group of students, they would provide a Hebrew teacher. A year after I graduated from college, a few friends and I began our Hebrew education with the aleph-bet. My near fluency in French often frustrated me: If the teacher produced a picture of a house, my brain said *maison* before the new word, *bayit,* surfaced.

By this time, having finished the prerequisites, I started my private M.A. program in Old Testament. I studied theories of biblical authorship, exegesis, and archaeology. When not writing papers, I continued to read the existentialist novels I loved. Often I struggled through them in French. But one evening a week, I dropped back to kindergarten level. More satisfying than earning an A+ on a graduate paper was unraveling the vocabulary and grammar behind those mysterious Hebrew squiggles.

On Friday nights, at Julian's request, I placed short white candles in the two-branched brass Israeli candlestick that was a wedding gift from a friend of his family. I lit them, recited the Hebrew blessing Julian had taught me, then read the English translation: "Blessed art Thou, O Lord our God, King of the universe, who hast sanctified us with Thy commandments and commanded us to kindle the Sabbath lights." My confirmation class teacher would be pleased, I thought, even though Mother thinks it's silly. But it was important to Julian and was beginning to feel right to me.

Julian recited the blessing over the wine, and then we ate, the flickering candles adding romance to the meal. Often we went to services after dinner. I practiced sounding out the prayer book's Hebrew words. More of a game than a prayer, it nonetheless helped his synagogue become mine.

8

I was a novice in more than just Hebrew language. There was the kitchen. Since my family had always had a hired cook, I hadn't learned at my mother's side. At first, I burned canned lima beans, under-scrambled eggs, and shot through the ceiling the day I tasted Tabasco sauce. So the night that I set a perfectly roasted pork loin on the table I was proud indeed. Until Julian came into the dining room.

"What's that?" he demanded.

"A pork roast," I answered.

In a visceral response that seemed to start in his toes and gallop up his body, he grabbed the platter and without a word stomped through the kitchen. I followed him outside to see him dump the roast in the garbage can.

"What have you done? Do you have any idea how hard I worked?"

His silence was thick and dark.

"And what about the shrimp in the freezer? You eat that. Your mother even serves shrimp." I was indignant. "And bacon! I've seen you eat bacon." He had never mentioned keeping kosher. His parents had dropped the dietary laws years before, after their parents died.

"If you expect me to be consistent, I'll have to become a Hasid," he retorted.

I wasn't sure exactly what a Hasid was, but surmised it was someone who was far more ritually observant than my Conservative husband. I knew I didn't want him to be one.

My stomach churned. Dinner was ruined, but worse, I had crossed an invisible line that apparently I was supposed to know about. I don't think Julian himself knew the line was there until he saw the pork roast on *his* table in *his* home. In the six years I had known him, I had never seen him more than mildly annoyed. Where was this unexpected and ferocious anger coming from? At the time, I had no idea; I just knew it was intimidating and scary. Looking back, it was as if he acted on behalf of every Lithuanian ancestor who had ever been attacked as a Jew.

What did we eat that night? Salami? Scrambled eggs? Or just the side dishes? Whatever we ate, that event, which we both remember vividly, was an enduring lesson in the emotional power of tradition—and in the wisdom of my parents' advice to always make up before going to sleep.

9

In June, 1964, Julian, who had left the department store with the intention to teach rather than practice retailing, and I received our degrees from Emory University. His was an M.B.A., mine, a masters with a concentration in Old Testament. As I walked down the aisle to receive my diploma, my black gown jutting out front as if concealing a watermelon, I heard someone whisper, "Do you think she's pregnant?"

I was, and two weeks later, I gave birth to Lawrence David Yudelson. When I summoned the nerve to peek under the receiving blanket, I was shocked to see that he looked like a scrawny plucked chicken. When we left the hospital, he weighed barely five pounds. Our pediatrician (who had taken care of Julian a generation earlier) recommended that we postpone the briss, the ritual circumcision, until the baby had gained a little weight. Julian consulted the rabbi, who confirmed that we must defer to the doctor's opinion.

A briss, with its ritual blessings and prayers, was not part of the Reform lexicon of that era; Reform babies generally underwent a non-religious hospital circumcision. But, aware of its biblical roots in God's promise to Abraham, I was eager for our son to enter the Covenant the traditional way. My parents didn't remember ever attending a briss and didn't consider it important. I turned to my mother-in-law, who graciously took charge. The ceremony would be in our home, with a deli luncheon to follow.

On our baby's 14th day (instead of the usual eighth), our home was filled with relatives, friends, and the mohel who would perform circumcision. Suffering from vicious headaches resulting from the anesthesia for my Caesarian section, I lay in bed and imagined what was happening in the other room.

During the endless wait, my head pounded in the rhythm of my baby's cries. What were they doing to him? Finally, the mohel placed the baby in my arms and said, in a voice tinged with awe, "In my entire experience as a mohel, no baby has ever watched me and listened so intently. He seemed to absorb every word."

"Oh, that must be because I spent the past nine months studying Bible," I replied in flippant relief that the procedure was over.

The mohel took me seriously. "That must be it."

Julian and I knew that we had produced the most brilliant baby ever, but we laughed at the idea that he had studied Bible *in utero.* Over the years, as Lawrence displayed a keen fascination with the Torah and Judaism, I began to wonder if the mohel's words might have been true after all.

When our son was two months old, we moved to Evanston, Illinois, a Chicago suburb, for Julian to pursue his doctoral degree in marketing. Arriving in a strange city during the 10-day period between Rosh Hashanah and Yom Kippur, we were delighted when Julian's cousin invited us for dinner and services. Imagine our surprise when we learned that their Reform congregation in Glencoe, Illinois, was so large that there would be a "triple header" for Yom Kippur Eve, with services at 6, 8 and 10 o'clock. Our hosts opted for the early service, to be followed by dinner in their home. As a Reform Jew who had fasted on the Day of Atonement every year starting when I was 10, I was taken aback by the thought of eating at least two hours after the holiday's onset. But new in town, knowing no one else, and not even knowing where there was another synagogue, we accepted.

Through the praying-hands-shaped windows, Julian and I watched the dazzling orange sun drop lower and lower until a single ray lingered in the growing darkness, a moving backdrop to the service that inaugurates the holiest day of the year. And then we went back to his cousin's home to feast, postponing our fast to fit their convenience. I found eating on the actual holiday so jarring that it negated what had been an awe-inspiring service. It made my Atlanta Temple seem downright traditional by comparison..

While Julian went to class and studied, I stayed home to care for our baby. I had ample time to read, and for the first time in my life, no assignments to complete. Books by Isaac Bashevis Singer, Bernard Malamud, Elie Wiesel, and others helped me fill major gaps in my understanding of traditional Jewish life and culture.

10

It's Passover Eve, 1965. We settle Lawrence with the babysitter, then drive from Evanston to Chicago's "gold coast." In the elevator to an upper floor of an elegant, high-rise apartment building, I feel nervous. What will I say to these kind hosts? Will I be able to follow their seder? Will I somehow embarrass Julian, who knows them from a study group the men attend?

"Welcome. Come in. This must be B.J.," Norman Asher greets us. "Helen, this is Julian, the young man from our Talmud group."

I smile, shake hands, and murmur my appreciation. After meeting the other guests, I look around. The living room is spacious, sophisticated, and inviting. We move toward the dining room, where the table, beautifully set with bone china and sterling silver, could be my parents' seder table except for the unfamiliar Haggadah at every place. Unlike the Union Haggadah, the abridged Reform version to which I am accustomed, this is the full, traditional Hebrew text with—thank heavens—an English translation. My nascent Hebrew is surely inadequate.

I'm relieved that our gracious hosts give us the opportunity to participate in English or Hebrew according to individual preference. I've never attended a seder that combines traditional text with modern discussion. The commentaries are interesting, the conversation intelligent. I hope that someday, when Julian and I host our own seders, we can bring the ancient stories to life this way.

By taking seriously the traditional opening words of the Haggadah, "Let all who are hungry come and eat," our generous hosts feed more than my body.

* * *

Julian had met Norman Asher when he stumbled onto a Sabbath morning Talmud study group. It was, he said, his first contact with laymen who were both Jewishly knowledgeable and worldly in their daily lives. At this time, I knew the Talmud only as an antiquated source in which I had "index-hopped" for graduate research. In spite of my focus on religion, I had grasped neither that generations of men had devoted years to its study nor that its legal and narrative interpretations of the

Bible shaped 20th-century lives. From Julian's weekly recaps, I learned that traditional Judaism filters the Torah through the ancient rabbis' lenses. Rabbis argued with each other across the centuries over the significance of every word and phrase. In the process, they transformed the Five Books of Moses from a "constitution" into a code of specific laws by which traditional Jews live. I found Julian's reports interesting, but they hadn't begun to change the way I saw the Bible: intellectually fascinating, even inspiring, but not a guide to daily life.

Nonetheless, we delighted in studying Bible together. Every Shabbat afternoon, while the baby napped, Julian and I read and discussed the weekly Torah portion. Week after week, we sought new insights from the English text we read to each other. In my course work, I had studied 19th-century Biblical criticism, the Bible's multiple authorship, and its relationship to surrounding cultures. I defended that approach to Julian, who preferred the traditional commentaries that assumed a single Divine authorship and probed every word for its deeper meaning. These rabbinic discussions dominated the notes of *The Torah: The Five Books of Moses* that he had given me as a gift. The inscription reads:

To בתיה [Batya, the Hebrew name given me by my first Hebrew teacher] *with love—a Hebrew Bible—may Torah & Judaism always be important in our lives. Julian.*

I lay on the living room floor, this new *Torah* open before me.

"Noah was in his generation a man righteous and whole-hearted; Noah walked with God," I read, then turned to the Revised Standard Version filled with handwritten notes from undergraduate and graduate courses. "Both translations say pretty much the same thing."

Julian glanced at the commentary in my new volume. "The rabbis raise the question of whether Noah was a good man only in his own immoral generation. Would he have been selected to carry on humanity if he had lived in a more righteous generation?"

"Either way, it's about his behavior, not God's capriciousness," I answered. "In the Gilgamesh epic, the Sumerian version of the flood, the gods chose Utnapishtim to survive the flood just because he was their favorite, not because he was better than anyone else. The contrast makes it clear what the Torah is saying."

"But it doesn't explain what it means to be righteous or blameless," Julian countered. And on it went, back and forth, until, invariably, contentedly sharing my love of biblical discussion with the love of my life, I fell asleep on the carpet.

11

One evening during our two-year stay in Chicago, a friend took me to hear a lecture by a rabbi whose name I don't recall—if I ever knew.

"We are all on a ladder of tradition," the speaker told us. He perched on a stool on a bare stage. His tzitzit—ritual fringes—dangled below his shirt, white against his black trousers. I knew even less about tzitzit than I had about separate seating for men and women when I was in France. Although they are clearly described in Exodus, I had seen the knotted strings only on the corners of a man's prayer shawl—and those only at the Conservative synagogue.

"In my case," he elaborated, "the issue may be whether the dietary laws allow me to order hot tea or only cold water in a non-kosher restaurant. You may be on a different rung. What matters is not where you are now. The important thing is to recognize that there is always a rung above you, and that you continually stretch to reach it."

Hot tea or cold water in a restaurant? This was an issue? I couldn't imagine such a thing. But climbing a ladder of tradition toward closer connection with God was an appealing image, even if it was at odds with the abridged version of Judaism in which I was steeped.

I had always known that Reform Jews observed only those rituals that they found personally meaningful. Now, eager to learn more about my heritage, I read a newly published book, *Abraham Geiger and Liberal Judaism*. Geiger and the other early reformers in 19th-century Germany were educated rabbis. Their proposal to drop rituals that they deemed outdated was designed to make Judaism more meaningful to their congregants' Enlightenment sensibilities. "With all its basic truth concerning the Unity of God and with all its noble ethical components," wrote

Geiger in a letter to a friend in 1836, "Judaism, partly due to nationalistic limitations and partly due to too great a stress on the ceremonial, has never been able to unfold a full religious life or to place itself on the summit of religious perception." It was time to drop hallowed rituals that were merely habit. I agreed that contemporary Jews—whether in Geiger's 19th-century Germany or a century later in America—should be allowed to choose the customs that enhanced their lives and to ignore those that didn't, especially those that set them apart from their Christian neighbors. All this seemed fine in theory. But, I wondered, how can I decide which rituals to keep when I was raised with such limited knowledge?

By the time I went to Sunday school in the 1940s and '50s, Reform Judaism focused almost exclusively on social justice as preached by the prophets. It had codified the *lack* of ritual observance rather than presenting options for people to choose. Traditional dietary rules—the laws of *kashrut*—were viewed as important to health in ancient days but irrelevant in an era of refrigeration and cleanliness. Reform Jews didn't refrain from work on the seventh day. No one I knew growing up lit candles or recited kiddush to welcome the Sabbath. My experience in the French synagogue demonstrated how the elimination of most Hebrew from services cut us off from other Jews.

As my Jewish world expanded, the condensed Sunday School edition no longer satisfied me. I began to resent Reform Judaism, especially its embodiment in my childhood rabbi, for handing me a step-stool instead of a ladder.

12

Granny, my mother's mother from Seattle, visited to meet her great-grandson. Granny had been a constant part of my childhood, spending several months with us each year. Coiffed white hair held in place with a thin net, manicured nails, and silk dress or wool skirt and blouse made her appear elegant; laced, low-heeled old-lady shoes gave her a no-

nonsense appearance. According to her whim and internal thermostat, we girls hopped up and down throughout dinner to open the window, close the window, turn on the fan, turn off the fan. But in the mornings, when I walked into the bedroom that I had given up for her, being with Granny felt cozy. While I rummaged through the closet for my school clothes, she sat in bed reading, a box of Pine Brothers honey cough drops on the nightstand.

"May I have one?" I would ask.

She handed me the box, and I usually took an extra. It was like eating candy before breakfast.

When I was young, she taught me to play gin rummy and solitaire, games that made me feel grown up. As I matured, we talked about books and current events. Now, in her late eighties, she was still interesting, demanding, and opinionated. We chatted while I changed Lawrence's diaper.

"How was Barbara Goldblatt's wedding?" I asked. I used to play with Barbara, the daughter of my mother's childhood friend, on youthful summer visits to Seattle.

"It was very nice," Granny replied, her voice beginning to prickle, "until they started doing that 'hora' dance."

I kept my eyes on the diaper I was pinning and my thoughts to myself. It struck me that a Jewish folkdance threatened Granny's status. Her parents had immigrated to the United States from Germany in 1849 and 1851. Unusual for her time, she had attended college and was one of UC Berkeley's first co-ed graduates, class of 1898. Like many of her generation, she considered Eastern European newcomers with their ties to the old world to be beneath her, an affront to her Reform sophistication and rationalism.

As I snapped Lawrence's overalls, I changed the topic to my young son. I knew that Granny would never understand that I was discovering beauty in the customs that she considered outmoded. Although her friends were Jewish, and she and my grandfather had been early members of Seattle's Temple De Hirsch, she seldom let Judaism intrude in her life. She couldn't possibly relate to the notion that I had stepped onto the ladder of tradition and was poised to dance up it.

In autumn 1965, during the harvest festival of Sukkot, we accepted an invitation to sit in a friend's backyard sukkah. The only sukkah I had ever seen was inside the Temple's sanctuary, covering the entire two-tiered altar: a magnificent green arbor crowned with leafy boughs and festooned with a colorful array of ripe fruits. After services, we children had trooped forward to receive a piece of fruit that the rabbi or a teacher plucked off for us. I remember the rabbi telling us that this represented the booths in which the ancient Israelites lived during their harvest festival. I don't remember hearing that an authentic sukkah belongs outside, that you must be able to see the stars through the roof, and that throughout the eight-day festival observant Jews eat all their meals in it.

With The Temple's extravagant sukkah as my framework, I was initially disappointed by the simplicity of our friends' structure: a temporary hut of unadorned plywood sheets topped with corn stalks. A card table held wine, juice, and cake. Metal folding chairs lined the three walls. The main decoration was our spirited conversation. Yet sitting in my first real sukkah, glimpsing the clear afternoon sky through the natural roof, I sensed a connection with those ancient Israelites that I had never felt as a child.

13

The following summer, 1966, Julian accepted his first teaching position at Marquette University in Milwaukee. We bought a house in a neighborhood festooned with swing sets and tricycles. While Julian settled into his work-and-write-a-dissertation routine, I worked to follow my sister-in-law's advice: "It's up to you to pursue friendships. People you'll meet already have friends, so call them as often as you need to until you become part of their lives." I joined Hadassah, National Council of Jewish Women, and the League of Women Voters. I befriended neighbors and did everything I could think of to meet people. Even though Julian's teaching schedule included twice weekly evening classes, I was seldom lonely.

On Friday nights, I lit Shabbat candles at the dinner table, Julian said kiddush, and we blessed a braided loaf of bread. After five years of marriage, it felt right to celebrate the Sabbath this way. After dinner, we put our two-year-old to bed, greeted the babysitter, and headed to services. We had chosen a Reform temple because I preferred the familiar prayer book and the predominance of English. Julian was most interested in the sermon, and Rabbi Weinberg seldom disappointed.

I still remember one sermon in particular. "Why deny yourself the light of the Sabbath candles?" asked the rabbi. "When you circle the lights with your hands and say the blessing, you acknowledge that God is paying attention. Imagine! The Lord of the universe cares what you do."

"Imagine!" I echoed internally. "This is a Reform rabbi speaking."

I couldn't envision the Reform rabbi of my youth saying such a thing. His religion, and that of the people I grew up among, seemed more intellectual than emotional or spiritual. We were discouraged from doing things, like lighting Shabbat candles, that would set us apart from our non-Jewish neighbors. And here was a rabbi from the same liberal tradition advocating it in a way that gave spiritual substance to my own practice. I was beginning to see that taking on more observance need not conflict with being a Reform Jew.

One February 1967 evening, as we greeted the rabbi after services, he looked pointedly at my protruding belly. "It must be soon now."

"I'm having a C-section in another 10 days," I replied.

"Best of luck. Julian, be sure to let me know what you have."

Whenever someone asked if I was hoping for a girl, I responded, "Nope. I'm hoping for a healthy." A girl would be lovely, of course, but healthy was what counted.

The following Friday night, three days before my scheduled surgery, Julian met Mother at the airport. When I heard the car in the driveway, I rushed to the door. Mom entered with a blast of frigid air, offset by the warmth of her hug. With a grin, she patted my portly tummy.

Julian toted her suitcase to his study, and we followed. "Mom, you're sleeping here. Bathroom's down the hall." I pointed. "That's Lawrence's room, and that's ours. I'll give you the royal tour in the morning." Eager as I was to show off our first house, I was just too tired to visit.

The next morning at 7, I entered her room. "Mother, wake up. I'm in labor. The frying pan is in the cabinet next to the stove, eggs are in the fridge. Diapers are under the changing table in Lawrence's room, and the diaper pail's in the bathroom."

Before she could answer, we were out the door. Apparently Ruthie was coming on her own schedule, not the doctor's and mine. Later that day, when I awoke from my C-section anesthesia, I held my precious daughter. Almost two pounds larger than her brother had been, she was perfect: smooth skin, blue eyes (which later turned hazel, like mine and my mother's), a shock of brown hair—and the determination to suck and suck until, a few days later, my milk began to flow.

Granny called to congratulate me.

"It's just like you to choose a biblical name." Her voice was uncomplimentary. "But," she added, "Ruth has always been one of my favorite names. And Leah..."

We had known that our choice of "Leah" for our daughter's middle name would please both families; my grandfather was Leo and Julian's grandmother, Leah.

Now my aggressive friendship campaign paid off. While I was home recovering from the Caesarian section and caring for an infant and a toddler, my new friends called and visited.

Julian, meanwhile, had sniffed out a Sabbath morning study group at a nearby Reform temple. After Ruthie was born, I sought a sitter so I, too, could study Torah with the religiously and professionally diverse group that Julian enjoyed so much. Saturday morning babysitters were hard to find, and I settled for a 10-year-old neighbor. The second week, I walked into the house to find both Ruthie and the young sitter crying uncontrollably. My baby, left unattended on a bed, had fallen. Though she was unhurt, after that incident I had no choice but to stay home and wait for Julian's second-hand accounts of the discussion. I don't recall that we ever considered that Julian and I might switch off weeks. This was the 1960s, and as a dutiful wife, I stifled my resentment that I was the one stuck at home.

With two children, we found it difficult to get out of the house on

Friday evenings. Saturday morning services seemed more feasible. By then, we had made friends with a couple 15 or so years older than we. I had first met Jane Klitsner at a Hadassah meeting at her home. She and I had discovered a mutual Atlanta friend, and soon she and her husband Marvin took Julian and me under their wing. Marvin had traveled the path from near-assimilation to traditional Judaism, and they encouraged our hesitant steps. Now they suggested that we join their Orthodox synagogue.

An Orthodox synagogue? Me? It was a weird thought. Partly because Marvin was a respected attorney, well-read, literate, and worldly—the reverse of my stereotype of Orthodox Jews—I agreed. But I wasn't comfortable with the prayers. I wasn't happy sitting with the women instead of my husband. I certainly wasn't at ease with the label. Yet I loved seeing Lawrence next to his daddy, contentedly turning picture book pages, even if to do so I had to peer over the mechitza, the divider separating the women's section from the men's. I was thrilled that my preschool son was eager to go to synagogue, week after week, even though he said that it was because he liked refreshments after services. He drank his weekly cup of orange soda while sitting on the rabbi's lap. This was a rabbi I revered so highly that I could barely utter two words to him, yet my little boy fancied sitting on his lap. So, despite my qualms, we stayed. I used to tell people that I paid dues to an Orthodox synagogue, but that I didn't belong. I was a Reform Jew who chose to add observances as I learned more about traditional options. Was there any place I belonged?

14

The table that extends the length of our friends' living and dining rooms is set with the familiar seder symbols. Four-year-old Lawrence's eyes gleam with anticipation. Ruthie, barely one, screams from a port-a-crib in the back room. How naïve to think that if I put her to bed at the usual time, she would fall asleep in this unfamiliar environment. She has no intention of missing out on the excitement. She yowls as if afflicted by boils, lice, frogs, and all the plagues we will recount later that evening. Finally, when I can stand it no longer, I bring her to the table. Hoping to encourage drowsiness, I give her a few sips of wine. Before long, a silly grin on her face, she hiccups around the room, her toddler's gait made more unsteady by the Manischewitz "sleeping potion."

Our hosts' teenaged daughter turns to me, and with an air of reassuring wisdom that bespeaks personal experience says, "The most difficult children make the best adults."

In 1968, I couldn't imagine Ruthie as a young woman. By the time I could, the irony of that remembered remark stung: Sadly, I would never find out what kind of adult my daughter might become.

* * *

In our religiously mixed suburban Milwaukee neighborhood, Catholic, Jewish, and the one or two Protestant families decorated for almost every holiday. Front doors displayed jack-o-lanterns in October, Indian corn and paper turkeys in November. Christmas wreaths, shiny hearts, bunnies, and Uncle Sams heralded the seasons. In this spirit, Julian built a giant menorah to hang on the front of the house during Hanukkah. The four-foot-wide Jewish star had eight bulbs that could be screwed in, one a night, until all eight glowed. With an electrician's manual in one hand and *The Code of Jewish Law* in the other, Julian wired it so that screwing in the shammash, the ninth candle that is used to light the others, turned on the other bulbs.

Our contemporary version of the traditional Hanukkah menorah delighted our Christian neighbors. Our Jewish neighbors were less enthusiastic.

"Did you have to make it so big?" asked one Jewish neighbor.

"It's very, uh, nice," said another in a tone that suggested embarrassment. I knew how such a blatant Jewish display would have discomfited my Atlanta family, but I was delighted with my clever husband's creation. At one time, I would have not only sympathized but identified with my neighbors' uneasiness. Now I was fully on board with a proud display of my family's Jewishness.

The first night of Hanukkah, Lawrence, Ruthie, and I bundled up to watch Julian turn on his masterwork. Eyes aglow, tingling with cold, we retreated into our warm house to light the traditional candles on the living room sideboard.

15

As members of an Orthodox synagogue, we paid attention to holidays that we'd barely noticed before. That October, on Simhat Torah, Julian marched and danced with the Torah scrolls, Ruthie on his shoulders and Lawrence waving a paper Israeli flag at his side. When the procession came close to the women's section, I joined the crowd that touched our prayer books to our lips, then leaned over to press them against the scrolls. A piece of me rankled at being shunted aside, but a larger piece delighted in my family's participation. Intellectually, I had known that on Simhat Torah Jews complete the annual cycle of Torah readings with the last section of Deuteronomy and begin anew with the first words of Genesis. But now the beat of Hebrew songs vibrated through my body. Our usually staid rabbi's dancing showed me what it meant to rejoice in the Torah.

A few months later in February or March came Purim, a day that commemorates the deliverance of the ancient Persian Jews from a plot by Haman, a royal vizier, to annihilate them. Two childhood memories illustrate what I had learned about Purim in Atlanta. One was a song that told the story in multiple verses:

Oh, once there was a wicked, wicked man and Haman was his name, sir.

He would have murdered all the Jews though they were not to blame, sir.

So today we'll merry, merry be...and nosh some hamentaschen.

The second was the Temple's annual Purim carnival, an event that was peripheral to the day's meaning. One year my Sunday school class had been in charge of the "house of horrors." Peeled grapes and cold spaghetti representing Haman's eyeballs and intestines had evoked squeals of disgust from the students.

Now I was ready to observe Purim as an adult and a parent. I dressed the children in costumes—Lawrence as righteous Mordechai and Ruthie, like all little girls, as beautiful Queen Esther. At synagogue, we listened to the chanting of the *Megillah*, the Hebrew scroll of Esther, a singsong backdrop to the English translation I read. Children were freed from the usual hushing of their parents; rather, they rattled noisemakers and hissed when they heard the name of Haman, the archvillain. Afterwards, they sashayed around in their costumes. With all of its drama and dress-up, it's no wonder Purim became Ruthie's favorite holiday.

My friend Jane, who had led us to her synagogue, introduced me to the custom of exchanging *mishloach manot*, gifts of food. Though I might have heard the Megillah read before, I knew nothing about this practice, based on a passage from Esther (9:22): "They [the Jews] were to observe [these days] as…an occasion for sending gifts to one another and presents to the poor." For the first time, I attempted to bake the traditional Purim treats, triangular, fruit-filled pastries called hamentaschen, to exchange with friends.

My first effort was a disaster. Hearing me rant about uncooperative dough, Julian strode into the kitchen. While Ruthie watched from her perch atop the portable dishwasher, Julian opened *The Joy of Cooking* to the page on pie crusts, perused the description, added flour to my sticky mess, and somehow made it work. His calm, superior air was maddening. Why was he so good at everything, even in *my* kitchen? And why, over the years, did he so often delight in reminding me that *he* made my first hamentaschen?

Half a year later, the High Holidays and Sukkot rolled around again. With warm memories of the sukkah we had visited in Evanston and the encouragement of our rabbi's wife, Julian and I decided to build our own. The neighborhood children watched, fascinated, from the backyard sandbox Julian had constructed when we first moved in, as he sawed and hammered according to the design he had sketched.

"What's your daddy building?" seven-year-old Christina asked Lawrence, now four, who enunciated few consonants when he spoke.

"A sukkah," he said.

"A what?" Christina assumed that, as usual, she simply couldn't understand him.

"A sukkah."

"Mrs. Yudelson, what's he building?"

"A sukkah."

"Oh."

One Sunday the family collected corn stalks for the roof from a nearby farm. Back home, I attached string to the stems of apples and grapes and stood on the picnic table to hang them from the wooden crossbars that supported the stalks. As usual, the neighborhood gang gravitated to the yard where the action was.

"What can we do?"

"I wanna help!"

"Let me, let me!"

I gave construction paper, scissors, and tape to the older kids, construction paper and crayons to the younger ones, including Lawrence and Ruthie. With giggly concentration, fortified by juice and cookies, they set about making decorations for our odd structure. After the children taped their paper chains, pictures of fruit, and scribbles to the walls, we all stepped back to admire Mohawk Road's first sukkah.

Holiday meals were an adventure in survival. I ran the clothes drier with the vent blasting hot air into our temporary structure. The wind whisked the warmth away while we huddled together against Milwaukee's raw autumn weather. Despite our discomfort, I rejoiced that I had climbed another rung.

16

As Lawrence approached kindergarten age, Marvin and Jane convinced us to send him to Hillel Academy. This was a Jewish parochial school that relegated the regular full school curriculum to half of the day and devoted the other half to Hebrew and Judaic studies. I wasn't sure about Julian's reasons, but my own were as clear as my memory of the

French synagogue: No child of mine would ever walk into a synagogue and not know where to sit.

Not long after we had made the decision about the school, we were visiting my family in Atlanta. Mother had invited Julian's parents and siblings to dinner. After the meal, the living room buzzed with simultaneous conversations. From across the room, Mom asked me when we planned to start speech therapy for Lawrence, whose obvious intelligence still hid behind a jumble of incomprehensible sounds.

"That's one problem with our decision to send him to Hillel Academy next year..."

Before I could complete the thought, the chatter stopped. Like an audience when the curtain goes up, everyone focused on my words.

"Hillel Academy?" someone asked.

"But you're such a strong supporter of the separation of church and state."

"What's wrong with your neighborhood school?"

I interrupted the barrage.

"Hillel won't offer him speech therapy, so we'll have to do that privately. But he'll learn Hebrew, and he won't have to go to religious school."

"But where will he meet Jewish girls?" asked one of my sisters-in-law.

"Why, at school, of course." Was this the only reason she sent her children to religious school, I wondered. And besides, my son wasn't even five yet.

My Reform mother addressed my Conservative mother-in-law in a stage whisper. "I wouldn't do it."

"Neither would I," agreed Julian's mom.

We had made a choice that would set us apart from our neighbors and take our children out of the mainstream. Perhaps our parents were also concerned that sending our children to parochial school would distance us from our families, even though we had no intention of letting that happen.

Hillel Academy turned out to be a family learning adventure. One day Lawrence came home wearing tzitzit, the ritual fringes I had first seen on the rabbi in Chicago. My friend Jane had warned me that when her son had been introduced to these biblically based fringes, he was led to believe that their holiness would protect him and he needn't look both ways before crossing the street. I anticipated a need to remind my son that they were a mitzvah, a sacred commandment, but not a magic spell—that he was still responsible for his actions. I was pleasantly surprised later that afternoon when Lawrence returned home from playing in his friend's backyard. "I started to do something naughty," he reported, "but then I saw my tzitzit and remembered that God cares what I do. So I didn't do it."

It was hard to object to the knotted strings hanging from a poncho-like undergarment when the message he had absorbed was not about blind (and perhaps unsafe) trust, but about living up to God's standards. Even so, it took me awhile to get used to seeing my son in this unfamiliar piece of clothing. Not surprisingly, my parents were less accepting of his untucked tzitzit and the *kipa* that he now wore all the time. (*Kipa* was the Hebrew word Lawrence had learned in school for the skullcap I had known by the Yiddish word yarmulke.) The next time we were together, they didn't say much on the subject, but I could read their distaste on their faces.

17

One evening, my aunt called from Seattle. "Would you like a Sabbath lamp that used to belong to your grandfather?"

"Heavens yes! Why me?"

I already knew the answer. My aunt's one child was no longer Jewish, and I had become the family's "religious fanatic."

The 19th-century Sabbath lamp proved to be almost identical to one my husband and I had admired in the Milwaukee Public Museum. A tapered, fluted vessel held enough oil to light a room far into the night, important for traditional Jews who did not make fire or light candles after sundown on the Sabbath. Originally the oil had flowed into arms that radiated to form an eight-pointed star. A drip catcher was hooked to the center point. Above, a chain of four rectangular links connected the oil holder to the top bracket and vertical central rod.. By the time I received it, a thick electrical cord almost obscured the chain, and small, round light bulbs had replaced the wicks.

When my mother saw the lamp hanging in our Milwaukee living room, she recognized it instantly, despite the new, less visible wiring and thin, flame-like bulbs. It had hung, she told me, in an alcove off the living room of her childhood home. She recalled that before joining his wife and children in the dining room on Friday nights—just another night for her privileged Reform Jewish family—her father would walk over to the alcove and click on the light. It was his one nod toward the Sabbath tradition.

I asked my grandmother, then in her lively, opinionated 90s, to verify Mom's little-girl recollection. "No such thing!" She remembered the lamp, but the Friday-night ritual had escaped either her notice or her memory.

My grandfather Leo, who died almost a decade before I was born and was only a photograph on my grandmother's dresser to me, must have been a forward-thinking man to electrify this lamp in the early 1900s. And yet, judging by my mother's account, he had clung to a piece of the tradition that had motivated his family to carry the lamp across the ocean from Bavaria to the far western shores of the New World.

This family heirloom became an important part of my family's growing Sabbath observance. On Friday afternoons I vacuumed the house and set the table with my good china. The children primped before the mirror in their Sabbath finery. Lawrence, and later Ruthie, stood on tiptoes to turn on the Sabbath lamp. At the table, I lit the candles. Past merged with present as I circled the flames with my hands to draw their light and serenity into my soul. Julian chanted kiddush over a goblet of wine, and we recited the blessing over the challah, two braided loaves of bread. During dessert, we sang songs the children chose.

"Lawrence, can you say those words more slowly?" We couldn't understand a single word of the song he had learned at school.

He repeated the words. The phrase that kept recurring sounded like "Big Gedalia Goomberg." What in the world was that?

I sent a note to the teacher requesting the words. Once she responded, we finally understood the story of the giant, Big Gedalia Goomberg, who stopped whatever he was doing when the sun went down on Friday. "Double, double, triple pay / Won't make me work on Saturday." After multiple verses of this offbeat paean to Shabbat observance, Ruthie chose a song, always the same. Week after week at our Shabbat table, the itsy bitsy spider climbed up the waterspout.

During one of my parents' infrequent visits in those years, we sat together at the Shabbat table. I lit the candles and recited the blessing in Hebrew and English. Julian launched into kiddush, preceded by the paragraph from the Bible describing the very first Sabbath. He followed the Hebrew with the English translation, "It was evening and it was morning the sixth day. So the heavens and the earth were finished..." (Genesis 1:31-2:1) Julian was comfortable with this prayer that he had heard every Friday night from infancy. My parents, on the other hand, twitched in their chairs until he finally concluded, "Blessed be You, Lord, who sanctifies the Sabbath." At the end of the meal, Dad, whose musical ear was better than our voices, grimaced good-naturedly through our off-key rendition of Big Gedalia Goomberg and the itsy-bitsy spider.

Later, while Mom read bedtime stories to the kids, Dad helped me clean up in the kitchen. "I don't really understand your Sabbath with all those rituals," he said, "but I can see that you have created a beautiful family feeling with it."

I turned from the sink to smile at him. "I really haven't moved so far away from you. Shabbat connects us not only to our tradition but also to each other. It's our way of living the values of family loyalty and love that you and Mom raised me with."

18

In 1970, Mom was in Milwaukee for Purim because our third child was due by Caesarean section the next day. I insisted that we distribute all our baskets before I would check into the hospital.

"Hurry up," Mother encouraged me. "It's almost time."

"We're near the end of the list," I assured her. "Just a few more and we'll be done."

For Mom, Purim was as irrelevant as Shabbat candles. Though I understood that she was afraid that I might "pop" at any moment, especially given my last pregnancy, it seemed to me that completing the mitzvah was a good backdrop to surgery. Even with our Purim deliveries, I made it to the hospital in ample time for my daughter Miriam's delivery the next morning.

In three years of attending the Saturday morning study group, Julian had developed a deep respect for Rabbi Brickman and was deeply affected when the rabbi's 14-year-old son died of leukemia the week that Miriam was born. One afternoon during my weeklong hospital stay—routine for Caesarian-section patients in those days—Mom left Lawrence and Ruthie with a babysitter (an older, more experienced neighbor than my erstwhile Shabbat morning one) and came to visit.

"What time is Julian coming?" she asked.

"He's not coming to the hospital tonight."

"He's not? What could be more important than you and the baby?"

"Being part of the *minyan* at Rabbi Brickman's." As a mourner observing shiva, Rabbi Brickman wouldn't leave home, even for services. Instead, a prayer service was organized at his house each evening.

"But there are others to do that, members of his congregation. He should be here with you."

"It's okay, Mother. I know he loves me, and I think he's right that he's needed there more." Elated by the birth of my second daughter, I didn't want to think about the enormity of the rabbi's loss.

Julian later told me that the close-knit members of the study group, many of whom were more traditional than Rabbi Brickman's Reform congregants, were the ones who showed up each night for minyan. The congregants surely visited, undoubtedly reached out and mourned with the rabbi's family, but they didn't understand the importance of helping constitute the prayer quorum that enabled the rabbi to say Kaddish for his son. By then I had learned enough to understand and accept Julian's priority. Much as I would have liked him at my side, I loved his compassion for a suffering friend and respected his desire to reach out in the way he found most meaningful.

When we drove up our driveway after my hospital stay, I was greeted by a beaming face peeking out of a blue-hooded, hand-me-down snow jacket. Lawrence was at school, Grandmommy waited inside. Ruthie raced into the house with us, all but knocking me over in her eagerness to see "her" new baby, (even though she hadn't seen me in a week). While I unwrapped the moving doll, Ruthie hovered, her three-foot-tall body radiating awe, love, excitement, and pride in being a big sister. I knew that her joy would be tempered somewhat when reality set in. But her expression at that moment is one that has stayed with me for more than 40 years.

Though often concealed by stubbornness and temper tantrums, the gratitude I saw on her face at her first glimpse of her new sister was an important part of her character. In Ruthie's baby book appear two prayers that she articulated in the following months:

"God bless Mommy, Daddy, Lawrence, Miriam, me, all my friends, all my neighbors, all my relatives, all the nice people, and all the mean people in the whole wide world. Amen."

"Thank you God for letting me play all day. Thank you God for letting me have so good food. Thank you God, thank you God, for letting me go to school. Thank you God, thank you God. Amen."

19

I became active in the Hillel Academy P.T.A., the one place where wives of Reform, Conservative, and Orthodox rabbis came together. At the end of one board meeting, Resa, a Reform rabbi's wife, said that she looked forward to the day when Reform Judaism opened its own day schools.

"A Reform day school? What would you teach?" asked Fagie, whose rabbi husband was Hasidic.

"Everything. How else will they know what they want to reject?"

Fagie looked taken aback, but Resa's response resonated with me. A

Reform day school could be true to the original reformers. It could teach children enough of the tradition that they could choose intelligently. They could decide whether or not to light Shabbat candles and say kiddush, whether to have one or two seders, whether to build a sukkah or celebrate Purim. Rather than the abridged version of my childhood, a Reform day school education could give students a full, open book, and they could choose which pages to follow and which to ignore.

But right now, I was more interested in what I might add than in what to reject. A conversation with my friend Helen, mother of one of Lawrence's Hillel Academy Orthodox classmates, had rumbled around in my head for months.

"How can you possibly take Saturday off?" I asked. "I seem to be running all the time, and you have one more child than I. How do you do it?"

"I'd be running all day on Thursday and Friday anyway. This way, I start my errands on Wednesday, I'm a little more frantic during the week, but you should see our house on Shabbos. I have time to read a story or play a game with each of the kids. On Saturday afternoon all four children nap, and so do I. It's so peaceful, if you came by, you'd think no one was home."

And then, as welcoming as she was practical, she invited the five of us for an entire Shabbat. I was astonished at her tranquil acceptance of housing and feeding not only two extra adults but also our three children in addition to her four—a total of seven youngsters ranging in age from under 1 to barely 6.

On the appointed Friday, we packed our clothes and drove across town with a combination of apprehension and excitement. How would it feel not to turn electric lights on and off, not to drive, not to hear the telephone ring—or to ignore it if it did—and to be guests in a situation that was strange to us?

Helen was right. Somehow on that Sabbath, we had time to pray, to play with each of the children, to read, and to converse as adults. But more important than the specifics of how we spent our time, and what we could or could not do, was the enveloping warmth with which my friend welcomed my entire family into her home. We learned that Shabbat hospitality is a hallmark of the Orthodox community.

Although we were not ready to observe the Sabbath the way Helen and her family did, we did turn it into a special day. No more errands. No more trips to the supermarket. Instead, we took our children on "Shabbat adventures" to parks, art shows, and special events. Without committing to the prohibitions against driving and spending money, we set Saturdays off from the other six days.

20

One day I told Helen that we'd love to have her eldest, Lawrence's best friend, spend the night, but I didn't know what I could feed him. "Oh, just wrap a couple of kosher hotdogs in foil and throw them on the grill. For breakfast, Cheerios and milk in a paper cup." Without letting her son eat from my dishes, she made kashrut, the dietary laws, which had seemed mysterious and difficult, sound doable. Without ever compromising her observance, Helen never let the details of the commandments get in the way of our friendship. The embrace of her outstretched arms was lasting.

Lawrence's kindergarten teachers created a classroom "store" that the English teacher used to teach simple math concepts like making change and the Hebrew teacher used to teach about kashrut and which blessings should be said for which food. When Lawrence came home from school seeking empty kosher food packages to stock the shelves, we discovered how much of our diet was kosher: fresh fruits and vegetables, eggs, French's mustard, Heinz ketchup, frozen vegetables, and more.

Nonetheless, I was totally caught off guard some months later when Julian turned down dessert. The plastic cloth under Miriam's high chair was littered with bits of meat. Ice cream dribbled down her chin onto her bib. Lawrence and Ruthie attacked their bowls more neatly.

"No ice cream?" I asked him. "I bought French vanilla just for you."

"I've decided not to eat meat and milk together when it's obvious," he answered.

"What? You just decided and didn't bother to tell me? And what do you mean by 'obvious'?"

"I mean I'm not going to read labels to find out if something has a dairy ingredient, but if I can see the meat and the milk, I won't eat it."

I was flabbergasted. And annoyed. Couldn't he have at least given me a little warning? I thought we were in this climbing-the-ladder thing together. I didn't appreciate his unilateral action, but, with little choice, went along as I shopped for the family.

Lawrence, who had learned about kashrut at school, accepted our changing diet more gracefully than I. The girls were too young to care. By then shrimp and other shellfish had joined that long-ago pork roast in the figurative trash bin. Now I found recipes to replace chicken cooked in cream of mushroom soup, a standard of the era. Julian said good-bye to salami and cheese sandwiches. We ate fruit instead of ice cream following a roast beef dinner. After a time, I decided that if we were going to do this crazy thing of not eating meat and milk together, we shouldn't be so casual about it. And so, despite my ambivalence and before I quite knew what was happening, I found myself checking labels to make sure there was no lard in the cookies, no milk in the hotdog buns.

On the one hand, it seemed easier to look for the kosher symbol than to read all the ingredients. On the other, what was I doing? Intellectually, the whole thing made no sense to me. For years, Reform Jews had attributed the injunction against pig products to health concerns that were no longer valid in the era of modern refrigeration. Now, my more traditional Jewish friends were telling me that it was all about keeping God's commandments. "Because He said so."

My mother had given her opinion on a visit to Milwaukee a couple of years earlier. We had enjoyed a long Shabbat lunch with Orthodox friends. The conversation must have turned to kashrut. Outside, before we were down the driveway, Mom pronounced, "Keeping kosher is barbaric!"

From my own biblical and archaeological studies, I knew that the whole division between meat and milk is based on a passage in Leviticus that states, "You shall not seethe a kid in its mother's milk." With dairy and beef cattle bred separately, how likely would it be that a calf would be cooked in milk from its own mother? And besides, I argued with myself, there was an ancient Hittite custom that involved boiling a kid in its mother's milk. So maybe the passage had been intended as an exhortation not to engage in pagan rituals and was no longer applicable in modern times. Either way, there was a lot of ground between the simple biblical injunction to the elaborate and Byzantine rules about separation of meat and milk, developed by the rabbis, involving multiple sets of dishes and cookware, waiting times, and care about the minutest ingredients. Surely, we could learn concern for animals' feelings—another reason often cited—without waiting hours between consuming meat and milk products. *This makes no sense*, I told myself as I perused labels in the supermarket. *I can't rationalize it*, I said as I threw out favorite recipes. *It's not the way I was brought up*, I grumbled in my head as I gave the kids juice instead of milk with dinner. But still...

Finally, even though it didn't fit my self-image, I decided it was time to get over my intellectual hang-ups. After lengthy discussions, Julian and I agreed that we would work toward making our home kosher. I consulted with our rabbi about what it would take to "*kasher*" my kitchen, and, in 1971, as we prepared to move to Cleveland, I began exploring the strange new world of keeping a kosher kitchen. I learned that items used with hot foods are *kashered* with heat, and so, piece by gleaming piece, I lowered my sterling silver flatware and serving dishes into steaming, boiling water, trying not to cook my fingers as I pulled items out with tongs that weren't quite long enough. To finish the procedure, I dunked the boiled items in a cold-water bath. I boiled metal pots and pans and replaced their plastic handles. I thoroughly scrubbed wooden bowls and glassware that had been used only for cold foods. I bought two new sets of dishes, one for meat meals, the other for dairy. As I kashered and packed, kashered and packed, I called friends for support and reassurance. Even as I changed Miriam's diapers or brushed Ruthie's hair, this strange, momentous undertaking was on my mind. Responding to my emotions, I had let something (Someone?) pull me up another rung. We had committed to keeping a kosher home.

21

Soon after we unpacked our dishes in Cleveland, I began to worry about my parents' Thanksgiving visit. I searched for words to tell Mom and Dad that our home was now kosher. I was used to pleasing my parents, and even though Dad had noted that our Shabbat dinners created the family warmth he valued, Mom's words about kashrut still echoed in my head.

"Mom thinks that keeping kosher is barbaric," I moaned to Julian. "How am I going to tell her? Will she think we're uncivilized or merely crazy?"

My parents arrived late Wednesday evening. Julian and I gave them a tour of our new home, skirting the kitchen. Sitting in our bold yellow family room over tea and cookies, I avoided the topic that was most on my mind. As we chatted about Julian's new job, the children, and our new neighborhood, I felt jittery about what we *weren't* talking about. They had survived our choice to send the children to a parochial school; they were accustomed, if not happy, to see their bright-eyed grandson, whom they adored, in his kipa and tzitzit. Mother and I continued to have unfettered conversations about philosophy, books, and babies. Dad and I cheered each other on. I didn't want this latest departure from my Reform upbringing to introduce a gap.

The next morning, I put the turkey into the oven and thought about breakfast for my guests. Mom, still in her bathrobe, ambled into the kitchen.

"What can I do to help?"

"First there's something I have to tell you about my kitchen." Now that I'd started, the words tumbled out, not at all as I'd rehearsed them. "We keep kosher now…." I paused while Mom picked her chin up off the floor. "We keep the meat dishes here, and there are the dairy dishes."

"Then you won't eat in our house."

To my relief, but not my surprise, she didn't want a separation between us any more than I did. Julian and I had discussed this aspect at length, and I could answer easily.

"Yes, we will," I assured her. "We're keeping kosher at home, but not out."

Mother mumbled something, then scurried out of the room and up the stairs to share this bizarre news with Dad. A few minutes later, she reemerged, dressed, and busied herself with her grandchildren. It was no doubt easier to focus on the tots than on her daughter's weird religious practices.

Over the long weekend and following months, Mom and Dad peppered me with questions: "Why are you doing this?" "Why is poultry treated as meat?" "How can you deprive the children of bacon and shrimp?"

Why? Because it feels right. Why is poultry treated as meat? Beats me, but it's part of the system. The children? They won't miss what they don't know.

I had known this would make no sense to my parents; my decision hadn't made intellectual sense to me. How could I explain something I barely understood myself? Only later was I able to articulate that maintaining a kosher home made me feel more complete. It was as if I had been precariously balanced on the far end of the thinnest tree branch. Kashrut gave me a sense of stability. It seemed to strengthen my connection with the trunk, the roots, and all the other limbs.

I didn't see my reconnection with this piece of history as a rejection of my parents, and I didn't want them to see it that way either. This was about finding my own place to bloom within their sheltering bower of love. It was about deepening my devotion to the religion they had taught me to be proud of. I simply had chosen to make religion a more intimate part of my daily life. Every time I planned a menu, every time I entered the grocery store, every time I fixed a meal, I was conscious of living my beliefs. And if my parents thought that their "favorite middle daughter," as Dad had always called me, was traveling backward through time to some primitive era, they loved me too much to say it to my face. Overall, despite their questions and my inarticulate attempts to explain, our relationship remained as comfortable and loving as it had always been.

22

"Ding-a-ling-a-ling. May I speak to Ruthie, please?"

Five-year-old Ruthie speaks into her pretend phone. "This is she."

"This is Mrs. Yudelson. Would you be willing to baby sit for Miriam while I finish cooking for the seder?"

"Yes, I'll be happy to," she says in her most grown-up voice.

For the past month I have been obsessed with preparing the house for Passover. In accordance with the biblical command "to remove leaven from your houses" (Ex.12:15), I have removed every crumb of leavened grain: half-eaten cookies from the toy box, breadcrumbs wedged between sofa cushions and frame, cereals and noodles from kitchen cupboards. It will be my first kosher Pesach—as Passover, I have learned, is called in Hebrew—and I have scrubbed and cleaned and made space for the newly purchased special-for-Passover dishes and utensils. I'll never finish in time with a two-year-old underfoot. As expected, Ruthie takes her job seriously and entertains Miriam until naptime.

Finally, I stand back to admire our new china rimmed with gold leaves and our sturdy goblets embossed with gold leaves. Considering how little we paid, they make a surprisingly pretty table. In the center is a Seder plate with a roasted egg, shank bone, horseradish, parsley, and charoset, a yummy mixture of apples, nuts, and cinnamon that represents the clay the Hebrew slaves used to make bricks. When the doorbell rings, Julian and I eagerly welcome his Cleveland State colleague and wife and lead them to the table. This is the first time we've conducted our own seder, and we're a bit nervous. Lawrence, who reads Hebrew more fluently than his parents, and Ruthie, ready to ask the four questions, sit expectantly. Miriam, too young to know what's going on, is cuddly and adorable in pajamas.

Julian begins. "Welcome to our seder. This is the first time I've led one, and I want to establish the ground rules. Really, just one rule: ask lots of questions. That way we'll have a lively, interesting evening. Remember, the only dumb question is the one you don't ask." We pour wine and grape juice, and Julian launches into kiddush. As prescribed by the Hagaddah, I bring a basin of water for him to wash his hands.

"What comes next?" he asks.

"Karpas," says Ruthie.

We pass the plate of parsley and the bowl of salt water. We each take a sprig and dip it into the salty mixture. I hand a piece to Miriam, who examines it from all angles. We say the blessing that thanks God for creating the fruit of the earth, then nibble our greenery.

"Who knows why we dip into salt water?" asks our leader.

Lawrence responds quickly. "To remember the tears that the Hebrews shed when they were slaves in Egypt."

When we finish munching our parsley, I lift Miriam from her highchair to take her to bed while Julian continues the story.

Later, as Julian and I clean up together, I compliment him for engaging both adults and children. He praises my turkey, the juiciest, most tender I've ever produced.

A few weeks later, we take the children to a hotel restaurant. The grilled cheese sandwich we order for Miriam comes garnished with parsley. When she dunks a sprig in her chocolate milk, Julian and I share a puzzled look, then exclaim simultaneously, "Karpas!"

* * *

When we moved to Cleveland in 1971, Julian and I took for granted that our children would attend a Jewish day school. In fact, we wouldn't have moved to a community that didn't have one. Now we had a choice: Hebrew Academy or the Agnon School. We explored both.

From the time Lawrence could talk, he had peppered us with questions about the universe. Starting with "Why is the sky blue?" and "What makes flowers grow?" he had graduated to queries about where babies come from, the origin of the solar system, and outer space. Religion was somehow different; he accepted without question whatever his Judaic studies teacher told him. Someday, we reasoned, he would probe that, too.

Hebrew Academy was an Orthodox school that followed a traditional split-day curriculum. We knew from our experience with Hillel Academy that Orthodox teachers love to present midrash, rabbinic explanation and folklore, with the same authority as the biblical text. I feared that our young son would be unable to distinguish between the text, which I revered, and those often far-fetched tales. When the time came that he would question the midrashic amplifications, would he end up rejecting the core wisdom as well?

Agnon was starting its third year. Its goal was to integrate Judaic and secular subjects. Few of its families and none of its teachers were Orthodox. All sought a Jewish education that would strengthen their families' Jewish roots without closing their children's minds to the world around them. That's what I was trying to do for myself, as well as for my children: create a vibrant and inquisitive Jewish way of living in the real world of 20th-century America.

We chose Agnon, and before long found ourselves among those parents pushing for more tradition. For example: We didn't think Lawrence should feel like an oddball for wearing a kipa in a Jewish day school; all the boys should be required to cover their heads. Kashrut was an issue because students all brought lunch from home, yet not every family kept kosher. Did a bologna and cheese sandwich, for example, belong in the lunchroom, where kids routinely swap food? Through Julian's position on the board and my PTA involvement, we urged the school to ban meat of any kind. Little did my new friends know how few rungs removed I was from my Reform background—that I had only recently begun to keep kashrut myself.

We joined Congregation Beth Am, the Conservative synagogue where the Agnon School met. Early on, we signed up for a family Shabbat retreat at a nearby camp. At the planning meetings, we began making friends with other congregants. We engaged in spirited discussion about the Shabbat morning *d'var Torah*, "word of Torah," or sermon. What would be meaningful to the adults as well as to our children, who ranged in age from teenagers down to our Miriam, not yet two years old? Batya, the Agnon School's art teacher, volunteered for the task. At the retreat, she delivered a d'var Torah in the ageless language of pantomime. Children and adults watched, enthralled, as Batya mimed weekday busyness. Calmness enveloped us as she paused, put aside her weekday pursuits, and lit her candles to usher the Sabbath Queen into her home.

That was the mood I wanted to create in *my* home—the mood evoked in Abraham Heschel's book *The Sabbath.* I had first encountered Heschel in college, and by now owned and had read several of his works. His writing was lyrical; his basic themes resonated with my spiritual quest. "When I marched [with Martin Luther King, Jr.] in Selma, my legs were praying," he had written in 1965. "The higher goal of spiritual living is not to amass a wealth of information, but to face sacred moments," he wrote in *The Sabbath.* I had lingered over his poetic description of Shabbat as a foretaste of eternity, a day when we leave behind the six days of space—days of creating, doing, possessing—to sanctify and dwell in time. "The Sabbath," he wrote, was a day to "understand that the world has already been created and will survive without [my] help." It's a day to connect with the deepest part of myself, to *be* rather than to *do.* His words moved me deeply and became the template for my developing Shabbat observance.

At the end of the song- and study-filled weekend retreat, Julian and I invited the group to study with us at our house the following Saturday afternoon. Every other Shabbat for the rest of the five years we lived there, six families gathered after services and lunch to study *Pirkei Avot,* a third century collection of rabbinic ethical maxims. While the adults and older children sat at the dining room table, surrounded by a variety of translations and commentaries, the younger children played. Periodically, they would run in, grab a piece of cake, and disappear again. We lived near each other, went to the same synagogue, and sent most of our children to the same school. Despite these similarities, our diversity of interests and experience made for amiable disagreement and lively learning.

23

A year or two later, Julian, the children, and I attended another Shabbat retreat, this one at a campground, where our synagogue group had reserved a section of campsites and a lodge for shared meals. After Shabbat morning services and lunch with our families, I wandered off with my friend Elaine. Not long after we moved to Cleveland, just about the time I figured out that her three children were the same ages as mine, she had come down with Guillain-Barre syndrome, an autoimmune disease that leads to muscle weakness and paralysis. Once she recovered from the yearlong bout, we discovered that we shared interests and values, the basis for a lasting friendship. That our children had become best friends was a bonus, and we often engaged in joint family activities.

Elaine and I settled ourselves on the ground under a tree. In one direction, a silvery pond reflected the gray-blue sky. In the other, tents showed green against the dark bark of the campground's trees. The shouts and laughter that broke the stillness were too far away to distract us with voices or words. A light breeze rustled the leaves and carried a hint of smoke from a campfire (not from our group, which followed the Jewish injunction against creating fire on Shabbat). I slapped at a mosquito that buzzed too close to my neck.

"Mmmm, smell that bacon," I said. "I can't imagine eating it anymore, but I still love the aroma. Takes me right to my parents' kitchen."

Elaine chortled. "I've never tasted it, but the odor turns my stomach."

We chatted awhile about the differences between growing up Jewish in Atlanta and in Brooklyn. Before long, the conversation shifted to more recent topics.

"In no time, I went from a tingling in my legs and arms to a heavy feeling to not being able to move," Elaine confided. "I was so sick that I was ready to record messages for each of my kids for fear that I wouldn't make it through."

My eyes filled with tears. I couldn't imagine being so near death. I couldn't imagine not living to help my children grow up.

"You're so lucky to be able to cry," Elaine said. "Tears have never come easily to me."

Too absorbed in the conversation for pretense, I didn't feign eye-watering allergies as I usually did. "What would you have said to them? What message could you possibly leave for such little children? Your youngest wouldn't even have remembered you." My eyes filled again.

I listened intently, no longer aware of the background noises, of the scenery, of anything beyond our conversation. She and I were one, speaking soul to soul rather than person to person, and somehow God was present in the conversation. Not that we talked about God, but that we were linked by an ineffable Being, what Martin Buber called the "eternal Thou."

The instant the experience became thought, the mystical three-way connection was broken. I became aware that my fingers were idly braiding blades of grass, that the sun was trying to poke through the clouds, that a breeze kissed my cheeks. Elaine and I continued talking, but what had been sacred was now, instead, an ordinary, albeit intimate, conversation between friends. I had studied Buber in college, written my master's thesis on his approach to history and biblical prophecy, and even taught an adult education course in Atlanta on his thought. But this unexpected perception of God's presence—not only in the wind and the sunlight, but especially in my bond with my friend—had moved Buber's words from my brain to my heart, an ephemeral experience dissolved by the act of intellectualizing it.

Led by Heschel and Buber, I was tiptoeing from the intellectual religion of my college years to a more emotional relationship with God and Judaism. I felt a greater sense of belonging—and a yearning to repeat the I-thou experience, which, paradoxically, can be experienced only in the absence of the effort to grasp at it.

24

In a Hebrew class at the Cleveland College of Jewish Studies, a gifted Israeli teacher helped me expand my meager vocabulary and encouraged me to carry on simple conversations. A classmate who worked for El Al Airlines helped Julian and me to plan a belated 10th anniversary trip to Israel.

First, we settled the children—now eight, five, and two—with my parents in Atlanta. Julian had been raised in a Zionist family, but my family, like many Reform Jewish families of that time, had no special feelings for Israel as the land of their people. Consequently, I was more amused than surprised to hear my mother's end of several phone conversations. "We're keeping our grandchildren while B.J. and Julian are in Europe." The exact words varied, but the theme was always the same: We were headed to *Europe*. The idea of Israel was so far from my mother's experience that she simply couldn't fathom it. The people she knew traveled to Europe. Israel? Not only a foreign country but a foreign concept.

In our three weeks in Israel in that summer of 1972, we connected with two thousand years of history. In Jerusalem, I rubbed my hands on the smooth stones of the Temple's ancient Western Wall, hoping to absorb some of its mysterious holiness. We removed our shoes to enter the Dome of the Rock, a mosque whose interior was far less impressive than its elaborate tiled facade that dominated Jerusalem's skyline. We explored the ruins of Masada, where 900 Jews committed mass suicide rather than succumb to the Romans. We climbed Belvoir, a Crusader fort with a stunning view of the Jordan Valley. We visited Yad Mordechai, a kibbutz just north of Gaza, where a relatively few determined fighters stopped the Egyptian army's advance toward Tel Aviv in 1948. In Haifa, we visited the Bahai temple. We admired Tel Aviv's cafes and modern life, and we sampled luscious Arab pastries in Jaffa. Although I had read extensively about Israel, its variety surprised me: mountains, fertile plains, and inhospitable desert; Tel Aviv's modern concert hall and Caesarea's ancient coliseum; its rich history and its embrace of modernity.

Our final week we explored on our own. One of the highlights was the night we drove in a rental car from Haifa to Tel Aviv. As darkness fell, Julian turned on the headlights. Drivers blinked their lights at us, signaling us that we had our brights on. Zooming down the highway, Julian searched with his toe for the dimmer switch. It was nowhere to be found. It was brights or no lights at all. Finally, we stopped at a service station, where no one spoke English.

"*Yesh ba-aya*," I told the mechanic, "We have a problem. Our lights (*menorot*, the word for lamp, not headlights), they are big and they are not small."

"*Rega*, one moment," he said, and motioned to us to release the hood. Not interested in a repair bill for a rental car, I tried again.

"Perhaps," I said in my juvenile Hebrew, "there is something inside the car."

"Ah." He walked to the door, reached in, and flicked the dimmer switch attached to the steering wheel.

I had done it! I had communicated in Hebrew. Triumphantly, we continued on our way.

The guided tour had taken us as far north as Dan on the Syrian border. On our own, we traveled to Israel's southernmost tip in the Sinai Desert, several years before it was ceded to Egypt. We flew on an Arkia internal flight, after a full-body security search, to a short paved strip amid vast barrenness. At the mountain that is usually identified as the place where Moses received the Ten Commandments, we half expected Cecil B. DeMille's thunder and lightning. The reality was more desolate than dramatic.

Julian summed it up for both of us. "If you can believe that 600,000 Israelites sustained themselves in this God-forsaken place, then believing in the revelation is easy." We didn't quite believe in either.

25

In October 1973, we sat in our Conservative synagogue, absorbed in Yom Kippur prayers. With Lawrence, Ruthie, and Miriam downstairs at children's services, I was able to worship with intention. Suddenly, the rabbi electrified the congregation with an announcement. Attacked on the holiest day of the year by Egypt and Syria simultaneously, Israel was at war. Julian and I turned to each other in horror and fear. We prayed with increased fervor. We imagined bullets piercing the Sinai Desert's barrenness. Even I, without Julian's interest in military history and in-depth knowledge of Israel's battle contours, could picture the area—the desolate hush that had awed us only a year before now broken by the frenzied movement of enemy tanks and soldiers.

Soon it was Sukkot. With several years of practice under his belt, Julian had designed a sturdy booth that fit snugly against the house, and was placed so that I could pass food through the kitchen window or the milk chute. We sat in the sukkah with friends, nibbling on dessert, bemoaning the length of the war. Unlike the 1967 conflict, which Israel had won in six short days, this one already had lasted more than a week, and Israel did not seem to be in control. Thoughts of Israel, its soldiers, and its citizens consumed us.

Before Israel ended the war, I baked a batch of challah, as I did periodically. My recipe normally created a sweet, somewhat heavy loaf. But never before had I kneaded like this. Over and over, I pounded the dough. I lifted it up, refolded it, and slapped it on the table. Vigorously. Purposefully. I vented my anger, angst, and acute fear for Israel, and in the process created the lightest challah I ever made.

I also played some of the best tennis of my life that October. My partners commented on my topspin, accuracy, and speed. Each ball was an Arab soldier; each drive another blow for Israel. It didn't affect the war effort, but it made me feel better. I hadn't known I cared so deeply.

26

In the mid-1970s, Elaine invited me to join her at an all-women's Shabbat retreat. In 1972, Hebrew Union College had ordained the first woman rabbi in the United States. A year later, the first Jewish feminist conference took place in New York City. Neither of us was an ardent feminist, but Elaine's husband was area director of the sponsoring organization. The sessions sounded interesting, and I agreed to go and to assist Elaine with planning and leading Shabbat services.

As a group, we welcomed the Sabbath with a typical Conservative service. Afterwards, a group of disgruntled females confronted us.

"This is a woman's gathering, and still you used nothing but masculine language."

"God of our *fathers*? Here, of all places, we should refer to God of our mothers!"

And on they raged.

Elaine and I were dumbfounded. Neither of us had ever felt rejected by the male-oriented language of prayer. But surrounding us were women who felt rebuffed by it. We would do our best to satisfy. Back in our room, we made a list of words we would substitute in the English. There was nothing we could do about the Hebrew, which is a gendered language with no neuter form. Those women who understood the Hebrew surely would recognize that we couldn't recreate the language.

The next morning, referring to our list, we substituted "God" or "the Divine" for "Lord," "God of our people" for "God of our fathers," and so on. After that service, smiling faces pressed in on us. The recurring, jubilant theme: "That's the first time in my life I've ever felt included in the prayers."

I attended study sessions, swapped views with other women, and heard lectures. But the most striking thing I learned was about the impact of the language of prayer. The only active participants in the services I had attended as a child were the rabbi, the professional choir, and the organist. We congregants chimed in for a few English prayers and responsive readings. One of three daughters with no brothers with whom to compete, and with a father who treated his wife and daughters respectfully, I had paid little attention to gender. If I had felt like an outsider, it wasn't because I was female. I had been as much a part of the Temple's passive congregation as any other child, or teen, or young adult. Later, in other settings, I had felt excluded by my ignorance of Hebrew language and traditional practices. That prayers might exclude women had never occurred to me.

The women at this retreat, however, felt alienated by the prayer book's male-dominated language. Worse, they felt that it failed to acknowledge their presence and individuality as Jewish women. They faced a tougher battle than I. They had to tackle centuries of a patriarchal religion, whereas I had already set about to include myself by learning and doing. But that weekend made me more sensitive to the effect of language on self-image, an insight that stood me in good stead much later as a communications professional.

It was a decade later that I encountered the prayer that observant men say each morning, "Blessed be You, Lord our God, King of the world, for not making me a woman." After my initial disgust, I began switching between the women's alternative printed in the prayer book, "Blessed be ... God ... for making me according to Your will" and my own heartfelt, feisty variation, "Blessed be ...God ... for not making me a man." Eventually my sense of empowered gratitude took over and I settled on "Blessed be ... God ... for making me in Your image."

27

Every Thanksgiving, my family gathered either in Cleveland or at my sisters' homes in New Jersey. Much as we loved being together, there was always tension. Leslie was an angry person who had never let go of her childhood resentment of me. In one middle-of-the-night-on-the-staircase conversation, she ranted about all that Mom and Dad had done wrong in raising her, as well as about my presumed injustices toward her. Finally I said, "If I did something to you when I was two and you were four, I apologize. But I'm not two anymore."

One Thanksgiving in Cleveland, Leslie, her daughter Rachel, Ruthie, and Miriam gathered around as I lit my Shabbat candles. Ruth and Miriam recited the blessing with me. Rachel, nine or ten, watched with rapt attention. Her large, expressive eyes reflected the dancing flames.

"Look at your daughter," I said to Leslie. "She seems to love this ritual." Rachel twirled in response.

Les scoffed. "Your kids don't seem so thrilled by it."

Knowing that any response would set off an explosion, I replied only inwardly: Why would my children react to a weekly ritual that was an essential part of their lives with the same excitement as Rachel, for whom it was a novelty? Neither they nor I could imagine our lives without Shabbat.

Julian and I continued to deepen our Jewish knowledge and extend our practice. By then, we began every meal with a blessing said aloud together. We began to sing the blessing after meals on Shabbat. Julian started a Shabbat morning study group at our synagogue. I took classes at the Cleveland College of Jewish Studies, focusing on Hebrew language and biblical texts in Hebrew. In 1973, with several other couples, we formed a monthly Saturday night "culture club" that became the only Cleveland setting where parents of Agnon School, Hebrew Academy, and public school students mingled regularly to discuss Jewish topics. We invited friends to share meals in our sturdy sukkah. We often had Shabbat guests, relished our Shabbat afternoon study group, and attended services virtually every Saturday morning. Lawrence, now eleven, co-led junior congregation services.

Saturday afternoon, when we weren't involved with our study group, was family time. At lunch, after kiddush and the blessing over bread, we read a summary of the weekly Torah portion and then discussed it. After lunch, we played endless games of backgammon, Landslide, Candy Land, and Memory. We went on "Shabbat adventures" to parks or art festivals. In winter, we took the kids sledding at a nearby park. We read, we talked, we played. I discovered the truth of what Helen had told me years before in Milwaukee: On Shabbat there was, miraculously, time to be with the family, with each child individually, and even have a few minutes left over for myself. Shabbat connected me with both my family and my community.

28

One evening after the children were in bed, Julian reported a conversation with a business school colleague, an Orthodox Jew, who adhered rigidly to *halachah,* the Jewish legal system.

"He told me that it would be better if the Agnon School closed and 160 students received no Jewish education if only one student would switch to Hebrew Academy for a Torah-true education."

I was shocked at this bigoted attitude. "I guess we Conservative Jews don't count in his book."

"He wants to show us what a 'Torah-true' Shabbos is like. After he checks with his wife, he's going to invite us for lunch. But we'll have to walk."

"Does he live nearby?"

"A few blocks past Temple Beth Am."

"Then we can drive there as usual and walk to his house."

It turned out the invitation was conditional on our walking the mile plus to our synagogue that morning, then to his house. Any driving would make us unacceptable guests. Somewhat offended, but curious, I agreed.

On the appointed Shabbat, Julian walked ahead with Lawrence and Ruthie. I followed at Miriam's four-year-old pace. After services, we continued to the colleague's home. Our host hustled us to the table and recited kiddush. We ritually washed our hands before he recited the blessing over the two loaves of challah and his wife served the meal. We had looked forward to a tranquil visit like the one we recalled with my Milwaukee friend, Helen. Instead, our hosts carped constantly at their bickering, rambunctious children. "Moshie, leave your brother alone." "Rivkie, share your toys." "I said stop." "No hitting!" "Can't you children behave?"

For this we walked three miles round trip? Had I expected too much? Had I expected a Shabbat based on Buber's sense of dialogue between people who respect and are open to each other? A Shabbat that reflected Heschel's idea of sacred time? No, all I had hoped for was a pleasant afternoon and the chance to learn something that might enhance our own observance.

It was obvious that adherence to our hosts' rule—no cars on Shabbat—was more important than any sense of *shalom*, peace. Had this been our first exposure to Orthodoxy, it probably would have been our last. We couldn't wait to get our children out of that poisonous atmosphere.

That Shabbat afternoon illustrated what I never wanted the Sabbath to be: a mere legalistic observance. Although that day was far from my mind when Dad was dying almost three decades later, I'm certain it laid the foundation for my response to his last request of me: Will you return to the hospital even if it's after your Shabbat?

29

A call from Ruthie's first grade teacher startled me.

"I don't know what's happened to Ruthie," she began. "Until recently, she's been a model student. But now she's picking fights and getting into trouble."

My bright, determined, enthusiastic Ruthie? "What do you think's going on?" I asked.

"I think she's trying to get herself moved into the other class to be with Hallie. One of the boys was recently switched for misbehavior. We think he'll do better with a different mix of children, but we're not going to change Ruthie. Would you please talk to her?"

That night, I sat on her bed.

"Ruthie, your teacher called today and told me that you've been getting in trouble at school." I waited for a response, but she looked away and held her breath. "Did you know that nowhere in the Torah does it say that you have to learn Hebrew?" Now she looked up, surprised. She was proud of her growing ability to speak and read the holy tongue. "But it does tell us how we're supposed to treat other people." I paused for this to sink in. "I know you're disappointed not to be in the same class as Hallie, but that doesn't mean you can say ugly things and fight."

I kissed her good night and left the room.

My parents had never cited words of Torah as a reason for me to behave properly—they were far more likely to reference Emily Post or Amy Vanderbilt. I was amazed by the almost magical effect. The behavior problem ended as quickly as it had begun.

By this time, we were strictly kosher at home but were more flexible elsewhere—if not as flexible as my parents might have liked. We never ate meat and milk at the same meal and had forsworn all pork and shellfish products. But away from home we ate beef and poultry that had not been slaughtered according to kosher laws, that was, to use the Hebrew term, "*traif*." "*Traif*," I used to say, "but not *traif traif*," my made-up term for totally forbidden animals.

On a visit to Atlanta in 1974, three years after I had dropped the "keeping-kosher" bombshell, we sat at my parents' dining table. Mother knew better than to serve us pork or shellfish, but she didn't understand that we avoided meat and milk at the same meal. We had finished our hamburgers (*traif* but not *traif traif*), canned beans, and mashed potatoes. Mom let Miriam, who was four at the time, ring the pewter bell that summoned Katie from the kitchen. Lawrence and Ruthie helped clear the dinner plates. Katie brought in dishes of ice cream and a plate of cookies. I noticed the three children exchange glances. They each took a cookie and, without a word or look from Julian or me, watched their ice cream melt. I was especially pleased that they did this silently, without chastising or embarrassing their grandmother. They had absorbed two messages: that our family keeps kosher, and that although their grandparents' practice is different from ours, we don't love or respect them any less because of it.

30

I answered the phone late on a January 1975 afternoon to my mother's voice.

"I'm having brain surgery to remove a tumor."

"You're *what?"* My head began a sympathetic pounding.

"They think it's benign, but it will grow anyway, so it has to come out."

Mom was such a young sixty-seven, so active, so healthy. "You seemed fine at Thanksgiving."

"I went to the doctor because I was having leg spasms. He suspected a tumor, and one of those new CT scans showed it."

"When's the surgery?"

"I don't know yet. I'll call you back."

In a shaky voice, I called Julian to the bedroom. I relayed the news, then asked him to take the kids to Arby's while I pulled myself together and waited for Mom's call.

When they returned, I sat in the family room, weeping, my sadness a bleak contrast to the cheerful gold walls.

"Go get ready for bed," I ordered the children. "First I need to talk to Daddy, then I'll tell you what's going on."

For once, with no arguments, they disappeared quickly. Julian sat near me, his expression mirroring my apprehension. "The surgery is scheduled for day after tomorrow. I've already made plane reservations for tomorrow. You'll have to deal with the kitchen and the carpools."

"Don't worry, I'll take care of everything here. You just go help."

Miriam, two months shy of five and the family dawdler, was the first one downstairs in her nightgown. Seeing my glum face, she stood on her tiptoes to kiss my moist cheek and said, "You'll feel better, Mommy, when your mommy feels better."

The next evening in Atlanta, Mom and I walked down the hospital corridor together. "I'm nervous about this surgery," she confided. "I've written Dad a letter, in case. I *could* die, you know."

I brushed aside her worries. "Oh, Mother, you're not going to die."

The following afternoon, when the surgeon came to the waiting room to tell Dad and me that the operation had gone well, we went out to dinner. When we returned to the hospital, we learned that Mom had not yet awakened from the anesthesia.

Until that moment, I had lived a fairy-tale life: loved by my family, respected by my peers, well educated, happily married, with three healthy children. Sure, there had been blips when I felt like an outsider, but I expected my life to have a "happily ever after" ending. Now I had to face a new reality: Mother might not wake up.

Dad, a realist by nature, called my sisters and Granny, Mom's mother, who had just turned ninety-seven. Dad and I went to Temple that Friday night to pray for her recovery. My sisters hastened to Atlanta from their New Jersey homes.

On my second visit to Atlanta, a few weeks later, I stood at Mother's hospital bedside, fighting back tears. Searching for words to fill the silence, I launched into a recent family anecdote.

"You know our storeroom in the basement? It's full of kosher cookie packages we brought back from New Jersey after Thanksgiving. We can't find kosher cookies in Cleveland, so we filled the entire back of the station wagon."

I watched her wave one hand before her face, examining it as a baby might.

"I went downstairs to bring a package up to the kitchen. I noticed an open cellophane pack. I confronted the kids, and they all denied snitching a cookie. But I was sure Miriam had done it—she's so mischievous."

It was hard to continue without an encouraging nod or "uh huh," but I kept going. "Miriam insisted she didn't do it, but I didn't believe her. A few days later, I found an open bag of flour and tiny white prints across the storage room. I knew Miriam wouldn't have opened a bag of flour, and small as she is, her feet are much bigger than those paw prints. So now we know the culprit: rats."

I shuddered dramatically, and Mom laughed.

"A whole family of big, ugly rats." I repeated my shudder.

Mom laughed again. Although the doctors and nurses had reported hopeful signs, Mother's laughter was my first indication that she was awakening.

Even after she was fully conscious, she never returned to being the vibrant woman who, just weeks before her surgery, had accompanied me to a Cleveland book club meeting. Without having read the book, she had contributed dynamically to the discussion. Undaunted by her change in circumstance, she worked fiercely, with the help of physical and occupational therapists, to walk and talk. But our new reality was that with no warning, she had turned into an old lady in a wheelchair, still sweet, still loving, but no longer the mother with whom I had shared a close, easygoing relationship.

Dad, though devastated, never gave up hope. When the neurologist said that therapy was useless, Dad insisted, and Mom finally did succeed in taking a few quad-cane-assisted steps and maneuvering up and down three or four stairs. This hard-won mobility, limited as it was, meant that she could get into a friend's house or make it through a doorway too narrow for her wheelchair. Dad learned to put Mom through her range of motion exercises and ended every session with what he called "KT," kiss therapy. Though his need to control drove the rest of us crazy, with her he was a model of devotion.

It didn't take me long to discover that Julian's ability to listen did not equal my need to talk about my distress. Fortunately, Elaine never tuned out my endless wailing and questioning. Why should anyone as active, generous, and considerate as my mother become so diminished? What justice was there in the world? As compassionate and helpful as Elaine, other friends, and our rabbi were, no one could give me back my mother or my storybook life.

That summer of 1975, as my parents' anniversary approached, I thought about their forty-year partnership. Mom was now fully dependent on Dad. Paralyzed on her right side, she couldn't walk independently or feed herself. Her speech was minimal. Instead of the travel and increased civic activities Dad had planned for his retirement, he was tied to the house as nurse, therapist, meal planner, grocery shopper, and social director.

I hesitated to suggest an anniversary visit lest Dad, drained by his unwelcome new life, snap at me. When, finally, I got up my nerve, I heard not rejection but relief in his voice. Perhaps it was on that trip, and maybe later that fall, that Mother managed to convey to me that she wanted me to go to Seattle for Granny's ninety-eighth birthday, since she would be unable to make her annual January pilgrimage.

I spent the first morning of that 1976 visit leafing through the scrapbooks that Granny, still in her "wrapper," as she called her pink nylon bathrobe, had dragged out of the closet. I probed for family stories, and she reminisced with a level of intimacy that was unusual for her. She paused at a photograph of Mother at about ten, a beautiful child with long, flowing hair. Wearing a simple dress, she stood poised next to her bicycle. Her eyes flashed impatience to resume her ride. My grandmother's small, delicate hands lingered on the page.

She sighed and said in a faltering voice, "Bertha was always so active."

I understood at that moment that although I was grieving for the vibrant mother who had turned overnight into an aphasic old lady, Granny had lost her little girl, her baby, a pain too deep for me to fathom then. We cried together most of that day, until Granny, true to form, announced, "Enough tears!" and returned the albums to the closet.

31

In the bicentennial summer of 1976, we moved from Cleveland to Rochester, New York.

"Rochester, *where*?" I had asked when Julian told me about the job offer from Rochester Institute of Technology.

While Julian completed a consulting contract, I packed. During our five years in Cleveland, our possessions had increased to fill every corner of our four-bedroom home. Now we were moving into a smaller house with the intention of adding on. As I stuffed toys and clothes into carton after carton, I worried. *How will we fit everything into the new house? Did we make the best choice? Is it the right neighborhood?*

I packed enough books to fill the U-Haul truck that Julian would drive to Rochester when he went for the house closing. Somewhere among the Jewish volumes, storybooks, retailing tomes, and contemporary fiction, I crammed my concern about uprooting Lawrence from school and synagogue just a year before his bar mitzvah. *Where will we find a synagogue we like as well as Beth Am? Will Lawrence be permitted to lead an entire service?*

In the basement, my nervousness slid into the spaces between the dozens of plastic model kits, probably more than Julian could build in his lifetime, that I stacked in cardboard boxes. *I hope he likes RIT better than Cleveland State. Building RIT's School of Retailing will be a challenge, but what will happen when the newness wears off?*

In the kitchen and dining room, I gently wrapped regrets at leaving close friends and laid them among double sets of dishes and silverware in the moving cartons. *Will I ever make a friend as steadfast and understanding as Elaine? How will I survive without her?*

To the children I expressed excitement, part real, part feigned. We talked about the adventure, the opportunity to make new friends, the letters we could write to maintain current friendships. Julian and I promised that soon after we moved, we would visit Elaine and her family, who had relocated to Boston a few months earlier. Ruth and Miriam were both excited at the idea of having separate rooms—no more squabbles over how much light at night or who touched whose things. Ruth eagerly agreed to the smallest bedroom if only it could be her own.

About a week before moving day, the ringing phone yanked me from sleep. Julian was already en route to his consulting job. Who could be calling at seven?

"Hello?" I answered tentatively, nervousness clawing at my stomach.

"It's Margaret. Leslie had a cerebral aneurysm last night. She's in the hospital. The children are at camp. Should I bring them home?" My sisters lived in neighboring New Jersey towns, and as the nearest relative, Margaret was the one to be called in an emergency.

"Huh?" My sister was asking my advice before I had processed her words. "Tell me again."

The second account jolted me awake. I thought of Leslie's son Paul, fourteen, and her daughter Rachel, ten. What to do? "The children have a father. Do you know how to reach him? Let him decide."

Our sister was divorced, and her former husband Dave, a symphony conductor, was in Europe. Over the next few days, Margaret—whose only child was not quite one—reached Dave, visited Leslie daily, and kept our parents and me informed. Four hundred and fifty miles away, I finished packing. Grief and fear for my sister left little room for moving day jitters.

A week after we arrived in Rochester, when we had barely found the bed linens and cooking utensils, Julian dropped me off at the airport to fly to Leslie's sickbed. He and the children drove to Boston for the promised trip to my friend Elaine's family.

Margaret met me at Newark. We hugged, but what was there to say? We went to the hospital to see our older sister. At 39, she lay scarcely conscious on the hospital bed, her long hair darkening the white pillow. "Oh, Leslie," I began and leaned down to kiss her. Silently, she looked at me. She raised her arm as if to touch me, but instead pushed me away. Stunned, I stepped back. Margaret walked over to her bed, and Les reached up with that same arm to pull her down in an embrace.

I had long known that my older sister was envious of me—perhaps for "displacing" her when she was two, or maybe for the seeming ease with which I navigated life and relationships. But to physically push me away?

This hurt me in a much deeper place than when she had conked me on the head with a baseball bat some thirty years before.

Margaret attempted to comfort me. "She's too sick to know what she's doing."

"I disagree. This is how she really feels. She's too sick to hide her true feelings under a patina of good manners and family expectations."

Back at Margaret's house, I called my friend Elaine for consolation. I cried; she talked. I ranted; she listened. I sobbed; she soothed. After an hour, or maybe two, of her wisdom, I was able to go back to the hospital. For the few more days I stayed, I visited my critically ill sister frequently with no further drama. After I returned to Rochester, Margaret told me that one of Leslie's friends, whom I had met during those days, had commented, "B.J.'s not so bad."

32

"This is the matzah of hope."

When I set the table this afternoon for our first seder in Rochester, I placed a fourth matzah under the required three that recall the ancient divisions of the Jewish population, still used today as the order in which men are called to the Torah: Cohanim (priests), Levites (priestly helpers), and Israelites (the rest of us).

Julian continues, "Who knows why we have a fourth matzah this year?"

"To remind us of the three million Jews of the Soviet Union, who aren't free," 12-year-old Lawrence responds.

Daniel, my friend Elaine's son, visiting from Boston with his family, adds, "The Soviet Jews can't celebrate Passover, or learn about their Jewish past, or teach their children."

Ruth, our eager Hebrew scholar, chimes in, "And they're not allowed to learn any Hebrew. Or anything else that's part of our tradition."

Julian picks up the thread. "Today they are persecuted for being Jews. This matzah represents our hope that someday they, and all Jews, will be free to hold Seders and practice Judaism."

The seder continues, but my thoughts are on my sister. Leslie is undergoing surgery to remove a malignant brain tumor, apparently in the same spot as the aneurysm that struck her nine months ago, just before we moved here. Her children, who now live in Rochester with their father and stepmother, are celebrating the seder with us, and each time my eyes fall on my nephew or niece, I feel fear on their behalf. Much as I care about the Soviet Jews, my concern for my sister is more pressing. Will she pull through? Will Paul and Rachel, who have already lived through their parents' divorce, also lose their mother? As I go through the seder rituals, serve the meal, and chat with my guests, hope eludes me.

* * *

On the fifth night of Passover 1977, Leslie died. My first reaction was physical: For hours, I trembled from head to toe. Finally the tears came. I cried for my sister, for her motherless children, and for the relationship that I wish we had had. I tried to remember the years when we had been close, when she, a college student, and I, still in high school, had exchanged weekly letters.

Eventually the questions set in: Why? Was there any meaning in her illness and death? Why did the aneurysm and tumor occur at the same spot? Did it simply mean that when your time is up, it's up, and if one thing doesn't take you down, another will? Did God have anything to do with any of it? Always in the past, where Leslie had gone, there went I two years later. The implications were scary, and the questions were endless and unanswerable.

Margaret and I remained in Atlanta with our parents for a few days after the funeral and our husbands' return home. With a strong need to feel sisterly, we moved into the same bedroom. One night, as we lay in the darkened room, Margaret confided, hesitantly, "You know those silver candlesticks that were Nana's? They were in one of Leslie's cartons that I brought to my house rather than put them in storage. I want to keep them, but I don't know if I should."

"No, I can't say I remember them, but why do you want them?"

"I've started using them to light Sabbath candles on Friday nights. But don't tell anyone; I don't know if I'll continue."

"You're lighting Sabbath candles? How come?"

"I needed some beauty in my life."

Though they were not mine to give, I assured Margaret that she should keep and enjoy Nana's candlesticks. And yes, I completely understood that lighting Sabbath candles could help dispel the darkness of an incapacitated mother and an older sister's too-young death. They could, indeed, bring beauty into one's life.

While Leslie had struggled for her life in a hospital and nursing home, I had been building a new life in Rochester. I had become friends with parents of my children's Hillel School classmates, and when my sister died, these families offered their support. One took care of Larry and Miriam while Julian, Ruth (who was close to her cousin Rachel), and I were in Atlanta for the funeral. Another left an entire Shabbat meal on my doorstep to ease my return to Rochester just hours before candle-lighting. These loving acts didn't resolve either my theological questions about my sister's death or our problematic relationship, but they made me feel cared for by my new community.

33

I had used our move to Cleveland as an opportunity to begin to keep a kosher kitchen. Our relocation to Rochester seemed like the right time to reach for a new rung. I decided that I would no longer eat any meat or poultry that was not prepared in a kosher kitchen. When I told Julian my decision, he responded with as much vehemence as if, fifteen years before, I had stuffed that pork roast into his mouth.

"But there are no kosher restaurants in Rochester. That means we'll never go out. It's ridiculous. You can't do it." His eyes were dark, his voice grim.

"I didn't say I wouldn't eat in restaurants. Just not meat. And why do you care what I order? I'm not telling you what you can or should eat."

"But you won't have much to choose from." He tried to sound rational.

"That's my problem, not yours. Almost every menu includes fish or pasta."

"But it will limit who we can go out with."

"Why?" I countered. "They won't care what I eat. Why should you? I've become uncomfortable with my level of inconsistency," I continued. "It seems strange to worry more about what I let into my kitchen than what I put into my body. I'm ready to climb another rung, and this is the perfect time. People I meet will only know me this way."

The "me" they would meet was not the unobservant Reform Jew Julian had married, not the somewhat meek Southern belle who had bent gracefully to his wishes. Seeking a new comfort level for myself, I risked moving beyond his.

34

While Julian settled into his teaching position at RIT, I helped the family adjust to our new city. I learned my way around when the contractors who were adding a bedroom and bathroom to our house sent me all over town to select plumbing and lighting fixtures. But the builders couldn't help with our most important decision: which synagogue to join.

In our fifteen years of marriage, we had belonged to Reform (Chicago), Conservative (Atlanta and Cleveland), and Orthodox (Milwaukee) synagogues. After "shul hopping" for a few weeks, we settled on Congregation Beth Sholom, an Orthodox synagogue that did not have a rabbi then.

This gave our son (who had requested that we call him "Larry" rather than "Lawrence" in our new home), the freedom to conduct as much as he wanted of the service for his upcoming bar mitzvah celebration. He decided to chant the entire Torah portion as well as the *haftarah,* the accompanying prophetic reading. He also wanted to lead *musaf,* the additional service for Shabbat, as would have been expected in our Cleveland synagogue. He was less enthusiastic about our insistence that he give a d'var torah, a short speech in which he would teach some of the things he had learned about his reading.

A Beth Sholom member suggested that we ask a congregant, Yale Potter, to train Larry. Yale's lined face radiated kindness, his humble words demonstrated true devotion to Torah. Evening after evening, Yale's careful, methodical voice drifted from behind Larry's closed door. Larry sang along in his higher-pitched, less tuneful, and less certain voice. After a time, Larry learned his readings and he had absorbed his teacher's confidence and meticulous attention to every word. I was pleased that he also seemed to soak up some of Yale's goodness and piety.

Relatives and friends from Atlanta, Cleveland, and elsewhere joined us for the bar mitzvah weekend in July, 1977. Shabbat morning we gathered in the sanctuary. The men and boys sat in the center. In general, I don't like the idea of a mechitza, especially when the women are relegated to a balcony or to seats behind the men's section. But the Beth Sholom mechitza separated in a way that encourages women's participation. From my seat on the side, raised a few feet and facing the men's section, I could see, hear, and participate. My daughters, sister, mother and mother-in-law, various other relatives, and a host of Cleveland friends sat nearby.

With the congregation, I stood and sat, turned prayer book pages, chanted prayers. But my head was churning about the details of the day. Was Mom okay? This was her first trip since her surgery two and a half years before. Would she manage the long morning? Had I seen to all of the details for the reception following services? Would the Beth Sholom members, who tended to descend on food like a pack of starving wolves, leave enough for my out-of-town guests to feel they had had a proper lunch?

When Larry rose to read from the Torah, I felt myself expand with happiness. Handsome in his beige plaid suit, barely visible over the lectern, he pointed to the beginning of the section he would read. He looked calmer than I felt while he waited for the blessing to be completed.

"A-men," he began. In a clear, high, assured voice, he chanted the Hebrew text that I had heard him practice for so many months. But this was from the parchment scroll, with consonants only, not the practice book that contained the portion both with and without the dots and dashes that constitute Hebrew vowels. This was in front of an audience, not alone in his bedroom, though his tutor stood nearby, a reassuring presence.

All the day's worries flew out my head. Now I felt only elation. Larry finished the first section, turned toward me, and grinned.

My sister-in-law leaned over to whisper in my ear, "He's wonderful!" I turned to look at my mother-in-law, who beamed. My mother's smile seemed pasted on, confused, as if she was having trouble processing this unfamiliar event. Thankfully I could leave any immediate needs to her nurse, who had traveled with my parents to Rochester and now sat beside her.

We had slated both grandfathers to be called up for an aliyah, to recite the blessings before and after a section of the Torah is read. Soon it was Grandpa Yudelson's turn. He rattled off the blessings as he had done hundreds of times, stood attentively as Larry read, recited the final blessing, and shook his grandson's hand. Once again, my son flashed me a huge grin.

When my father was called for the sixth aliyah, I held my breath. He came from a congregation in which only the rabbi knew Hebrew. Dad had learned the blessings from a tape Larry had made. He climbed to the podium, stood beside Larry and opened his mouth, but before he could begin, the rabbi started reciting a Hebrew prayer. Men surged forward to give him names to include in the prayer for the sick.

Poor Dad had no clue what was going on. We never thought to warn him about this, and it must have seemed as strange to him as a witch doctor's healing ceremony. I wished I could telegraph a message to him, but he took his cue from Larry and waited. Finally, Larry signaled him to recite the blessing. In his charming southern drawl, he managed the Hebrew flawlessly. Larry read the portion, they embraced, and Larry beamed me another smile.

"I love the way Larry smiles directly at you at the end of each aliyah," a friend murmured.

Throughout, my son exuded self-assurance, exhilaration, and, at the conclusion of the Torah reading, relief. Love and pride surged through me as he chanted the haftarah and conducted musaf. Was this impressive boy really bone of my bone, flesh of my flesh? I kvelled in his Jewish knowledge, which already was superior to mine, and rejoiced in the certainty that this ceremony did not represent the end of his Jewish learning but the celebration of a milestone in an ongoing journey.

35

During our first year in Rochester, the children had gone to Hillel School, a school that billed itself as a community school but was Orthodox in practice. The autumn following Larry's bar mitzvah, with only three other students enrolled in his eighth grade class, it was clear the time had come for him to leave the intimate environment of a Jewish day school. His sisters were having good experiences at Hillel, but he needed more classmates to challenge him academically.

Larry didn't make his transition to public school easy on himself. He marked his acceptance of the commandments by deciding to wear a kipa all the time. This ancient tradition of Jewish males, which shows respect toward, and humility before God, felt natural to Larry. He had always worn a kipa in his Jewish schools and at services. But to wear it all the time in public school? To mark himself as different at an age when fitting in already is such a source of stress? Concerned about his adjustment to the larger social world of public school, I was squeamish. Impressed with his commitment? Yes. Comfortable with his decision? No. But that was my dilemma, not his.

Until, that is, he actually started school that fall. One classmate, a known bully I later learned, used to snatch the kipa from Larry's head when they passed in the hall. Another, a Jewish boy, the only eighth-grader Larry had known before school began and whom he selected as lab partner, made it clear that he wasn't interested in friendship. When Larry finally worked up the courage to ask him why, he replied, "That was before I knew you'd be wearing a kipa." I had let Larry label himself as an outsider, even though I knew how uncomfortable that could be. Was it realistic to try to teach my children to live with a foot in both the

Jewish and the secular worlds?

I wanted my children to have the knowledge to feel confident and competent in any segment of the Jewish world, a skill I had lacked as a child and was working to gain as an adult. The endless dinner table conversations about Dad's involvement with Community Chest and Atlanta Family Service and Mom's work with League of Women Voters, though boring at the time, had impressed on me the importance of civic participation. I didn't want my children to give up that expansive universe for the particularistic Jewish world. This is America, I thought, where they can have their kosher cake and eat it, too.

36

Larry responded to that unhappy (and academically boring) 8th grade year of public school by asking to go to the Talmudical Institute of Upstate New York. During the year, in addition to taking a couple of courses at the community Hebrew high school, he had studied Talmud with a TIUNY student. The rabbis were eager to enroll him.

Rabbi Davidowitz paid a recruiting call. Julian and I learned that the secular subjects were taught by certified teachers who came to the sixty-student school after a full day of public school teaching. It was an old-school yeshiva: The boys studied Talmud most of the day; secular studies were an afternoon afterthought. But we knew that Larry was bright, motivated, and would learn no matter what. Our greatest concern lay elsewhere.

He surely would become more observant. Would he start telling us what we could and could not do in our own home? Would his version of Orthodoxy be like that of Julian's Cleveland State colleague? Would he begin to put the ritual commandments ahead of the ethical, the minutiae of kashrut and Shabbat observance ahead of honoring his parents and respecting all people? How would I handle it if he became like the family in whose home we had had that uncomfortable Shabbat lunch?

I remembered that as a kindergartener at Milwaukee's Hillel Academy, Larry had declared that we *had to* eat gefilte fish on Rosh Hashanah. He had informed me that if I didn't wear a white dress on Yom Kippur, I wasn't "being good." It was one thing to deal with the literalism of a five-year-old, who translated class discussions of what some people do on holidays into "thou shalts." It had been easy to say, "When you're a daddy and have your own home, you can do what you want. For now, you're a little boy in my home, and Daddy and I make the decisions."

But now he was, according to Jewish law, a "man" of fourteen. We had placed him on a ladder of tradition. Did I have the right to stop him if he chose to scamper up while I plodded behind?

I sought a way to pose our concern to the rabbi. "Recently, Miriam came home from school upset. On the bus, one of her second-grade friends, I believe it was your Lea"—I tried to sound nonchalant—"told her that if she didn't keep all the mitzvot"—the commandments—"then she was a bad person. I told Miriam to tell Lea that what Lea did was between her and her parents and God, and that what she, Miriam, did was between *her* and *her* parents and God."

The rabbi's face was impassive. Not a twitch, even when I mentioned his daughter. Julian and I exchanged a silent signal before I continued. "We're willing to let Larry attend the yeshiva, since that's what he wants, and we'll pay the tuition. But the first time he tells us that we're wrong for the way we practice Judaism, we'll yank him."

The rabbi nodded in agreement. Larry enrolled in TIUNY.

We delivered the same message to Larry: "Think what you want to think, but not a look, not a word about what we do." Larry abided by our rules, but before long he respectfully asked me to light Sabbath candles before sundown rather than at the dinner table, whatever time that happened to be. Cautiously, he let me know that the chicken needed to be cooked at least halfway, not just in the oven, before Shabbat began. Little by little, he nudged me toward a more precise Shabbat observance, always so that he could participate with us and still meet the expectations of his yeshiva rabbis.

I was the buffer between Larry's embrace of all that his rabbis suggested and Julian's wariness. The kitchen was my realm, and I quietly met my son's requests. Sometimes I groaned, sometimes I smiled, but

I found that the presumed inconvenience always enhanced my Shabbat observance. Besides, I figured, many boys Larry's age were addicted to alcohol or other drugs. His near-total absorption in religion seemed a far healthier form of teenaged rebellion.

However, like my mother, who had refused my request to light Shabbat candles, I had my limits. I put my foot down when Larry told me the rabbis said he should wear a black hat for daily prayers. Covering one's head was a custom rooted in the Talmud, where it is written, "Cover your head in order that the awe of heaven may be upon you." In medieval Europe, black hats were the head covering of choice. I saw no reason for my fifth-generation American son to emulate old world sartorial habits. And besides, I thought young boys looked ridiculous in black fedoras. I suppose, too, that I was concerned about his marking himself as even more of an outsider when he walked out the yeshiva's doors.

"Do you want God to listen to you or laugh at you? I'm not spending my money for a pretentious black hat for a fourteen-year-old kid. Absolutely not!"

Eventually he came home with a brown fedora purchased by one of his rabbis in what I supposed was a gesture of compromise. I pictured God looking down and laughing at a chapel full of swaying black hats, a lone brown topper breaking the monotony.

37

After Larry's bar mitzvah, in anticipation of Ruth's bat mitzvah three years later, we switched our membership from the Orthodox Congregation Beth Sholom, which had no clearly defined tradition for girls, to a Conservative synagogue, Temple Beth El. We joined the five hundred regulars who showed up every Saturday morning for services.

After a year or so at Beth El, Julian and I yearned for a more intimate, participatory service where our children would feel welcome to worship at our side rather than in a separate children's service. With five other families, we formed a *chavurah,* a circle of friends, to worship and celebrate together. We rotated homes for our biweekly ritual, going to Beth El the interim weeks. At the chavurah services, we each had the opportunity to set the mood through a description of one of the prayers, conduct the services, or give the d'var Torah. Julian and I left the task of leading prayers to those with greater Hebrew fluency and better voices. We took our turns at preparing Torah discussions that we hoped were inspirational or provocative for our congenial "congregation." On alternate weeks, we worshipped at our large, formal synagogue.

"Hurry, Mom," Ruth said to me one Shabbat in early 1979. "I don't want to be late for the Torah reading."

Her sixth grade class had just finished studying the week's portion, *Mishpatim,* Laws. For weeks I had listened to Ruth's enthusiasm about the in-depth discussion of how to treat slaves captured in war, an owner's responsibility for the actions of his livestock, treatment of widows and orphans, and other laws that formed Judaism's ethical underpinnings.

Just as we sat down, opened the book containing the Torah in Hebrew and English, and flipped to the right page, the reader began chanting from the Hebrew scroll. I read the English translation; Ruth followed the Hebrew text. During the recitation of the concluding blessing, Ruth turned to me.

"That's it? Thirty minutes? After we spent six weeks on it?"

How I envied Ruth's comprehension of the Hebrew and her grasp of the details of the portion. Although I had read it numerous times, I had never studied it with the rabbinic commentaries. My daughter's explanations taught me that I shouldn't gloss over this and similar sections as legalistic and boring. By reading the notes that accompanied the text, I discovered rules relating to honest testimony, respect of property rights, and sexual morality—laws that are basic to a functioning society. I found compassion toward the poor and the stranger—an idea that I had always credited to the prophets. No wonder these four chapters had occupied Ruth's class for six weeks.

As Ruth's bat mitzvah approached, we met with Cantor Rosenbaum to set a date. The typical Beth El bat mitzvah consisted of the girl's father being called to the Torah for the final aliyah. With his daughter at his side, he recited the blessings before and after the Torah reader chanted the section. Then the bat mitzvah girl chanted the blessing before the haftarah, the haftarah itself, and the final blessing. If, as was often the case, there were two bat mitzvah girls that morning, they split the reading, one reciting the blessings before and one after. My determined, competitive daughter knew that she could do anything her brother could. She was not about to settle for half a haftarah reading. We asked if there were other possibilities, and the cantor explained that it would be possible to have an all-women's service. Men could be in the congregation, but I, not Julian, would have an aliyah. The only other family that had considered this approach had backed off when the father objected to not being called to the Torah.

Earlier, Julian had made clear his position on women in Judaism. He had proposed the board motion at our Cleveland Conservative synagogue to make women equal to men in all aspects of congregational worship. Now he conceded graciously. "I had an aliyah at Larry's bar mitzvah. This time it's your turn."

Ruth was jubilant. We set a date in June 1980, several months after her February birthday, when Rosh Hodesh, the new moon, which marks the start of the next Hebrew month, would fall on a Sunday. Shorter than the Sabbath service, the Rosh Hodesh service is more involved than an ordinary weekday service. It includes a short Torah reading and Hallel, a group of psalms. Rosh Hodesh is also a celebration that historically has been celebrated as a women's holiday. Ruth would lead the entire ceremony.

As a Hillel School student, Ruth had never attended afternoon Hebrew school. Now she faced Beth El's required Bar/Bat Mitzvah class on Sunday mornings. I picked her up after the first session. One look at her red face and flaming eyes and I asked, "What's wrong?"

She erupted. "The cantor, that's what! He thinks we don't know anything! He said that we would learn about Shabbat, about holidays, and all sorts of stuff I already know. He talked to us like babies. He said something about work and what is and isn't allowed on Shabbat, and he was wrong. Finally, when I couldn't take it any longer, I raised my hand and said, 'There's a difference between work and *melakha*'"—the Hebrew word the Torah uses for labor prohibited on the Sabbath—"'and it depends on which you mean.' He agreed with me but said that most in the class don't know that distinction. I'm not going back. I'm not a dummy, and I don't want to be treated like one. I can't stand him!"

All this before we were out of the parking lot. I took a deep breath and turned to her. "You have a choice," I said calmly. "You can put up with Cantor Rosenbaum and have an extraordinary, one-of-a-kind bat mitzvah service. Or you can decide you can't stomach him and not have a bat mitzvah. It's up to you."

I was confident which she would choose. Most mornings between then and the June bat mitzvah, I awoke to the cantor's taped voice chanting the Rosh Hodesh service in the room where Ruth was brushing and curling her hair.

Our next negotiation with Cantor Rosenbaum was to get Ruth excused from attending Shabbat services at Beth El, normally a requirement for the months leading up to her bat mitzvah. Larry had stopped driving with us to Beth El. Instead, he walked to Beth HaKnesses HaChodosh, an Orthodox synagogue where the yeshiva rabbis worshipped. Ruth had followed her brother, and she, too, preferred the smaller, less pretentious congregation and service. By then, she had earned the cantor's respect, and he agreed that she could fulfill her requirement at a different shul.

38

We are near the end of the seder that marks Passover of 1980. This one has been such fun. For the first time, our chavurah group is doing it together—less work for all of us plus the camaraderie of good friends. I doubt if I've ever laughed so much during a seder. I love seeing how much the children know, how comfortable they all are with the Hebrew prayers and rituals, and how eagerly they join in the discussions. And how wonderful to be with people who know melodies for Hallel and can carry a tune! It's just dawned on me that these prayers are part of the Shabbat morning service. I wonder why I never made the connection before.

"Baruch atah … borei p'ri ha-gafen." We bless the fourth and final cup of wine. As we sip—by now I have switched from wine to grape juice—someone asks why we drink four cups. The children, most of them Hillel School students or graduates, jump in with their answers. "They symbolize the four verses of redemption mentioned in the Bible. 'I will bring you out, I will deliver you, I will redeem you…' I can't remember the fourth." Another child chimes in, "'I will take you to Me for a people.'"

We read together, "Ended is the Passover seder according to custom, statute, and law. As we were worthy to celebrate it this year, so may we perform it in future years. O Pure One in heaven above, restore the congregation of Israel in Your Love. Speedily lead your redeemed people to Zion in joy."

We break into song. "L'shanah ha-ba-ah b'Yerushalayim." Next year in Jerusalem! Ruth sings with gusto, expressing her deep longing to visit Israel. Someday, I think, when she's older…

And now comes my favorite part, "Who Knows One." Darn, I wish I could keep up with the Hebrew.

"Sorry, guys," I say when they have finished, "but I have to do at least the last verse in English."

I start, "Who knows thirteen? I know thirteen."

Others join in, "Thirteen attributes of God. Twelve tribes of Israel." We pick up speed. "Eleven stars in Joseph's dream. Ten commandments." Now I'm in childhood mode, determined to finish first. "Nine months of childbirth. Eight days of circumcision. Seven days of the week." People drop out, laughing. "Six sections of the Mishnah. Five books of the Torah. Four matriarchs." Only Ruth matches my pace. "Three patriarchs. Two tablets of the covenant. One God of the world." Ruth and I burst into laughter. I think it's a tie, but the consensus is that Ruth beat me by half a syllable.

We go home happy, satisfied, free of worry, and unaware that this is Ruth's last seder.

* * *

While Ruth prepared for her upcoming bat mitzvah service, I planned the festivities: casual Shabbat meals for out-of-town guests and a catered backyard open house on Sunday afternoon. I found a guitarist to accompany Ruth and her friends in Israeli song and dance. The invitation expressed Ruth's deep commitment to God and the Jewish people with the well-known quote from "her" book, Ruth: "Your people shall be my people, and your God, my God."

Beforehand, friends offered to pray for a nice day for us. "Save your prayers for something important," I replied. "If it rains, our un-air conditioned house will be crowded and sticky, but Ruth will be wonderful, we'll be surrounded by family and friends, and if people are too miserable they'll just leave."

They should have prayed for Ruth's voice. She awoke that Sunday morning with laryngitis, brought on, no doubt, by excitement and fatigue. Fortunately, the microphone amplified her whisper. When it came time for the Torah reading, I chanted the blessings and listened proudly to my talented, spirit-filled daughter read about the sacrifices offered in ancient days in honor of the New Moon.

B.J. and Ruth

The portion was an ironic contrast to the groundbreaking changes that Ruth's bat mitzvah represented; Beth El had voted only days before to allow women to be called to the Torah. The idea was so new in much of Conservative Judaism that when we had urged Julian's mother to have an aliyah, she had refused. She was from the old school, which left those things to men. But Ruth danced boldly into the future, eager to claim her role as a knowledgeable Jewish woman.

Ruth, Julian, and B.J. at the backyard bat mitzvah party

And I? How did I feel as the parent who had an aliyah at Ruth's bat mitzvah? I know I was nervous before I chanted the blessings and relieved when I had finished. No doubt my head was full of the details that accompany the planning of such a day. And despite my earlier disregard for weather, I hoped that the light rain would dry up in time for our outdoor party.

But beyond that, try as I might, I cannot recall what it meant to me then to be standing beside Ruth as she read from the Torah. Surely I kvelled in this child-woman who had a strong sense of herself and an equally strong sensitivity to other people, who was a serious student and a fun-loving friend. I would hope that gratitude filled me for the miracle of a daughter who, once she had outgrown her toddler tantrums, brought me immeasurable pleasure. But what I want most of all to remember is if, standing beside Ruth to recite the ancient blessing historically reserved for men, I felt a special connection to God.

If I did, that delicate memory is gone—overwhelmed, no doubt, by the emotional weight of what followed eight months later.

Larry, Miriam, and Ruth

39

Those next months were happy ones for our family. Ruth spent the summer at Camp Ramah, her favorite place on earth, where she prayed overlooking the lake, spoke Hebrew, deepened friendships, starred in her unit play, and became a sailing skipper. Miriam, now ten, enjoyed day camp. The annoying little sister and the "lord-it-over-her" big sister were happy to be apart. In order to skip 11th grade at TIUNY, Larry, who generally stayed out of the girls' squabbles, took a six-week summer school English course at a nearby private school and learned more about literary analysis than in all the rest of his pre-college years combined.

That fall, Ruth went to public school for the first time. Despite her pre-first-day jitters, she quickly enlarged her circle of friends to include new classmates. Miriam continued at Hillel School, where her closest friend was the daughter of a yeshiva rabbi. Larry was making plans to attend an Israeli yeshiva the following year and applying to colleges for the year after that. Julian, director of RIT's School of Retailing, taught classes and spent hours reading student papers. I was a student at RIT, moving steadily toward my master's degree in instructional technology.

My Jewish observance had settled into a comfortable rhythm: Shabbat dinner with the family, Shabbat morning services either at Temple Beth El or with the chavurah, Shabbat afternoon with the family, holiday observances with friends, and kashrut as a daily reminder of my Jewish choices. On the High Holidays, I walked rather than drove to services. One year the girls and I slogged through a downpour to Rosh Hashanah services. Our laughter and singing turned the soaking walk into an adventure.

Although she attended holiday services with Julian and me, Ruth had made a place for herself at the Orthodox congregation. Most Saturday mornings, she popped into my room after Julian had left for his regular Shabbat morning study group, Larry had left for shul, and I still drowsed in bed.

"May I wear your locket today, Mom?" or "How does this outfit look?" or merely, "I may not be home for lunch; the Kamins have been asking me to go there."

Groggily, I would respond affirmatively, though not without a tinge of dread that she'd be out of touch all day. None of the people she'd be with used the phone on Shabbat. Although I trusted her and her friends, I wasn't so certain about the rest of the world.

That Hanukkah, five sets of candles glowed in our breakfast room. From the time in Milwaukee that Larry had come home from Hillel Academy's kindergarten with a hand-made menorah, we had each lit our own. Mine was my mother's Hanukkah gift to me the year I was engaged. Julian's was an antique store find. The children's were all handmade, inventive designs of clay or wood, using bottle caps or metal nuts for candleholders. Each night of the eight-day holiday, we lit the candles and sang the Hebrew blessings and other Hanukkah songs in off-key "harmony." Then Julian stepped outside, in snow boots and muffler, to light the outdoor menorah that had traveled with us from Milwaukee to Cleveland to Rochester.

Hard as I tried, I never succeeded in interesting my family in my father's tradition of naming and betting on the candles. However, one evening during Hanukkah 1980, a delighted Ruth almost levitated from her chair when she unwrapped a monogrammed crew neck sweater. My mother's custom of a gift a night ... what child could resist?

40

That winter, Ruth had a dilemma. The National Conference of Synagogue Youth's regional convention was going to be in Utica, N.Y., on the same early February weekend as the Camp Ramah winter reunion in Toronto. Which should she attend? Her brother was an NCSY chapter leader. Finally old enough to join, she had eagerly attended meetings and had loved the first convention she'd attended in Binghamton that fall. On the other hand, she missed her camp friends, with whom she corresponded regularly.

"Well, most of your camp friends live too far away to visit often," I said. "You just can't get to Kitchener or Hamilton or Toronto that easily. Why don't you go to the NCSY convention? You'll meet kids from all over upstate, kids you'll see several times a year at conventions. If you want to get together for a Shabbat in between, it'll only be a one- or two-hour bus ride away."

"Yeah, I guess that makes sense," she agreed.

When I signed Ruth's and Larry's permission forms, I couldn't have found Utica on a New York map. I just knew it was closer than Toronto.

They were both delighted to miss school the Friday of the convention weekend. I took them to the Beth Sholom parking lot, where a chartered bus waited. They immediately headed toward their friends.

"Wait! Come back here. Let me give you a hug. Have a great time!"

"Shabbat shalom," they smiled, hugging me quickly, and dashing toward the bus.

At home, I prepared for houseguests who would arrive soon from Michigan for their nephew's bar mitzvah. That evening, conversation turned to a recent string of serial murders of young children in Detroit.

"It's been unspeakably awful," someone said. "The whole area's terrorized."

I shuddered. "I can't imagine how a parent survives the death of a child."

We sat in silence a few moments, then said our good-nights and headed to bed.

In the middle of the night, the telephone pierced my dreams. I reached for the phone, but it wasn't by my bed. I followed the insistent ring to the next room, groping in my semi-stupor for the receiver.

"Hello?"

"This is Laurie Green. I'm in Utica with NCSY. There's been an accident. A drunk driver plowed into a group of kids walking to their hosts' homes. Ruth's in the hospital."

"Oh no," I moaned. "What's wrong?"

Julian rushed to my side. "Ruth's injured," I snapped. "Get on the downstairs phone."

"What about Larry?" I asked.

"He was in the same walking group, but he wasn't hit. He's OK."

Julian picked up the other receiver. "Who is this?" he demanded.

"It's the regional advisor," I cut in. "I recognize her voice. It's not a prank. Laurie, what's wrong? How is she?"

"Two other girls have died, but Ruth's going to be okay. She's our baby. We'll take care of her."

My throat constricted.

"The doctors need your permission to remove her spleen."

I couldn't speak.

"Do we have a choice?" interrupted Julian from the other phone.

"Not really."

"Then the doctors have our permission to do what they have to do," I croaked.

"You'd better come right away," Laurie urged before disconnecting.

I hung up and dialed a close friend, a neurologist. "Ruth's been in an accident. She's in the hospital in Utica. We've given permission for them to remove her spleen. What have we done?"

His sleepy voice was calm. "You've done the right thing. Call me when you know more."

We dressed hastily, threw a change of clothes into a bag, grabbed Ruth's favorite stuffed animal, awakened our houseguests, and quickly recounted the little we knew.

"We're driving to Utica right now. Take care of Miriam."

"Do you have any cash on you?" our guest asked. When I shook my head, no, he found his wallet and handed me money for tolls and gas.

Dazed and worried, we climbed into the Buick station wagon that Ruth had dubbed "Fancy Schmancy" because it was our first car with automatic locks and windows. Julian steered toward the Thruway. Streetlights lit the roadside slush, and the familiar street seemed longer than usual. Finally, we were on a nearly deserted highway heading east toward Utica. Julian stared at the road, his face rigid with concentration and what I presumed to be fear. Only green exit signs broke the emptiness of the moonless night. We tried to talk, but what was there to say? Only questions. What would we find? Would Ruth be OK?

Finally, I broke the silence. "What's a spleen, anyway? What will it mean not to have one?"

"I think you can live without it."

We whizzed by a rest stop. The car seemed to hurtle past exits, yet the time between landmarks felt interminable. As we approached Syracuse, my stomach suddenly lurched. Like the sensation when you go over the top on a Ferris wheel. Ruth loved that feeling. I glanced at my watch: 3:20 a.m. "I think something terrible just happened," I said. "I have this horrible feeling that she's not going to be OK."

Until this moment I had been too dazed or panicked or just plain naïve to think ahead. But now the reality of Ruth's peril began to sink in.

Julian, focused on getting us safely to our daughter, didn't answer.

We reached the Utica exit, paid our toll—why was the clerk so slow?—and followed signs to St. Elizabeth's Hospital. By then, fear had settled like a mound of cold, dirty slush in my stomach. Julian parked near the emergency entrance, and we raced inside.

"We're Ruth Yudelson's parents," I shouted to the first person I saw. "Where is she? Is she all right?"

Laurie Green materialized with a doctor. "Come with me," the doctor said. He led us toward the ICU. "It's worse than we thought," he said. "The force of the car destroyed her brainstem. She's in a coma." I could tell from Laurie's face that she hadn't known this.

Julian and I clutched each other. Stunned. Broken. Trying to absorb the incomprehensible. "Can we see her?"

The doctor took us to her bedside. Despite the tubes and monitors, Ruth looked peaceful. Asleep. In a gentle voice, the doctor said, "We don't expect her to recover."

I sobbed into Julian's chest. His body was rigid as if the slightest movement would shatter him. Finally, I pulled myself away.

"Ruth…" I turned to the doctor. "Can she hear me?"

"Maybe. Talk to her, stroke her. It will help you, and it may help her."

I leaned over and gently kissed her forehead, wetting her hair with my tears. After minutes, or hours, or days, I searched out a pay phone to call my doctor friend.

"Her brain stem is damaged, and she's hooked up to all sorts of tubes and things," I said. "We don't even know what questions to ask. Would you call the surgeon and make sure they're doing all they should?"

I waited until daybreak to call my father. How could I tell him that his granddaughter was not expected to live? I couldn't, but of course I did. And I asked for his telephone credit card number (a rarity in those days) so that I could make unlimited calls from the hospital pay phone.

Later that morning I sat in the cafeteria with Julian and Larry. "I was right there," Larry said. "When some of the kids moved into the street because the sidewalk was unplowed and slippery, I didn't. It didn't feel safe to me. All of a sudden, a car appeared from nowhere, and bodies were flying. Someone called, 'Cover them, cover them.' I tore off my jacket and ran over to someone lying in the street. I reached down to cover her." He steadied his voice. "And saw that it was Ruth." With trembling hand, I tried to bring my tea mug to my lips but gave up. Larry twiddled with a fork and mumbled, "The scene keeps playing in my head."

I didn't know how to comfort my son.

41

When we returned to the hospital Sunday morning after a sleepless night at a motel, two black-clad figures stood outside Ruth's room. Rabbi Jablon, at whose synagogue Ruth led a Shabbat congregation of young girls, and Rabbi Kamin, from the Yeshiva, whose daughter Ruth had tutored. They had taken the 2 a.m. train, the first one after Shabbat, to be present for us and for Ruth.

Midway through the next week, the rabbi from Beth El called to ask if he should come. "A congregant is able to fly me over in his private plane." He had to wait until someone could fly him there?

"No, don't bother," I told him. I wanted to be surrounded by people who loved Ruth. Who cared. Who would take a middle-of-the-night train. I had no patience for someone whose own convenience came first.

Well-intentioned nurses told me that when God goes into His garden, He picks the most beautiful flower. Small comfort: I hadn't asked for the best and the brightest; I wanted Ruth, my daughter. Here. With me.

Friends who drove from Rochester to offer comfort and support told us that dozens of people in the community were meeting nightly to pray for Ruth. They changed her name to Ruth Chaya—Chaya means life in Hebrew—because of a belief, dating from the Middle Ages, that a name change would baffle the Angel of Death, who summons people by name. Others seemed impressed by this community outpouring; I just wanted Ruth to get well. Did God answer prayers? How could he, if the doctors were right that she would never regain consciousness or brain function?

One day, at a relative's behest, I asked a particularly sympathetic ICU nurse a question, although I was pretty sure I knew the answer. "Have you ever seen anyone this seriously injured leave the hospital alive?"

She looked down, took a deep breath, looked me straight in the eyes, and said, "On rare occasions, but they leave no better off than when they arrive. You don't want that for Ruth."

During that week, this same nurse told me that Ruth had her period. Just a month before, I had quietly helped my daughter celebrate her entry into womanhood. The irony of this sign of life on her deathbed was unbearable.

Each time I entered her room, the crucifix on the wall above Ruth's bed felt like an assault on my soul and my being, but I was too immobilized by grief and despair to do anything about it. Had I been a Christian mother waiting for her child to die, I might have found comfort in a crucifix as a symbol of God's loss of his own son. But for me it was a reminder of the generations of Catholics who had blamed my people for Jesus' death. I was undoubtedly far too distraught to consciously recall the way my sixth grade teacher had mortified me for being Jewish or the long-ago discomfort of singing Christmas carols in public school. But at a visceral level, I wanted that Christian symbol gone. I hated the thought that Ruth's richly Jewish life had started at St. Michael's Hospital in Milwaukee and now was ending, decades too soon, at St. Elizabeth's in Utica. A kindhearted friend must have sensed my discomfort and finally reached up, unasked, to pluck the offending icon off the wall and tuck it out of sight.

I spent hours in that small room, watching Ruth's heartbeat dance across the monitor in a hypnotic pattern that testified to her strong heart—despite the fact that her brain, her essence, was dead. I thought about how upset she would be by her chipped front tooth—her only outward injury—and prayed for strength to endure. When not with Ruth, I sat on the corridor's linoleum floor under the lone pay phone, seeking solace from friends and relatives.

Julian had returned to Rochester to prepare final exams for his students (how did he have the strength?), and that wall-mounted pay phone became our daily connection. Larry had gone back to school. Friends had brought Miriam to us that first weekend, and then she too had returned home, to school, and to friends' houses every afternoon until Julian picked her up. My friend Elaine, who now lived in Miami, had flown up to wait with me.

On Shabbat—a week after our lives were shattered—Elaine and the Utica rabbi's wife prayed the morning service in Ruth's hospital room.

"I can't even see the words," I mumbled.

The rebbitzen responded, "The rabbis say that the gates of heaven are opened by tears."

If so, those gates should have swung open wide. My copious tears fell on Ruth's comatose body, while the fervent prayers of Elaine, who loved Ruth, and the compassionate rebbitzen flowed over and around us on their way heavenward.

During the twelve days I waited with Ruth, Cantor Gartenhaus, the NCSY advisor, returned to Utica. He pulled me away from my unresponsive daughter's bedside to walk and talk and walk some more in the stinging February air. Back at the hospital, he sang to Ruth. In a plaintive voice, he crooned, "[The Torah] is a tree of life to them that hold fast to it, and all who uphold it are happy." Although I knew the Hebrew words, I had never heard this melody. It was, he told me, Ruth's favorite.

By telephone, my parents, sister, and friends grieved with me. Julian's parents and siblings were in touch either with him or with me. All I remember for sure is that the phone was both my lifeline and my tormenter. How many times could I sob the same despair, the same hopelessness into the black receiver? When Miriam began having nightmares, friends brought her to visit again, but this time I wouldn't let her see her sister, whose face had puffed into a caricature of itself. I didn't want my little girl to carry that image.

Sometime during that awful eternity, Rabbi Jablon contacted Rabbi Moshe Feinstein, America's leading authority on Jewish law, to discuss if and under what conditions we could discontinue life support. Rabbi Jablon arranged for a Rochester neurologist—not our good friend, who felt too close to Ruth to perform this service—to come to Utica to examine her.

I waited in the corridor outside the ICU. His grim face told me everything. Before he could speak, I said, "I can survive whatever I have to, but I can't be mother to a Karen Ann Quinlan." Quinlan, whose case had made national headlines, had lived for years in a "persistent vegetative state" after being disconnected from life support.

"There is no similarity to Karen Ann Quinlan," the doctor declared. "She always had some brain function. Ruth has none."

"You didn't know Ruth," I muttered, tears coursing down my cheeks.

"My children knew her. And I saw her last week in the Hebrew High production of 'Mame.'"

In other words, he knew how full of life, how talented she was. And now he was telling me that there was no chance that she would ever breathe on her own—much less sing, act, dance, read, or even feed herself.

Soon after, Rabbi Jablon informed us that from a Jewish perspective, we could remove her from life support. But the notoriety of the Quinlan case meant that the Utica doctors would not proceed without a court order. After long-distance consultation with Julian, as the on-site parent, I had to sign the court petition. It was simultaneously the easiest and hardest act of my life. Ruth's spirit had long since escaped her body, and I had permission from the highest rabbinic authority. I recall that my hand was steady. But as soon as I formed the last letter, my whole body—every muscle, tendon, and ligament—trembled with despair. I had just sealed Ruth's death.

Once the petition and court order had been processed, (an hour? a day? two days?), a hospital nurse found me sitting at a table, trying to read, turning pages without comprehension, my friend Elaine at my side. The nurse placed her arm on my shoulders and asked gently, "Would you like to be in the room when we disconnect her?"

To my everlasting regret, I declined the opportunity to hold my daughter in my arms when she took her final, machine-aided breath on February 18, 1981.

42

Assorted relatives and friends came to Rochester for the funeral, held, according to traditional Jewish practice, the next day. An endless line of stricken faces filed past to murmur comforting words—words I was beyond hearing. What could anyone say? What words could undo the work of the drunk driver? I remember a rabbi telling me that because this was Purim Katan, a month before Purim in a Jewish leap year, eulogies were inappropriate. He and the other speakers would not extol Ruth, just speak the simple truth about her full, short life.

Rabbi Jablon, with his red beard and kind eyes, told the overflowing crowd how responsible Ruth was, how caring and giving, loved by all the children in the junior congregation she led at his synagogue. She was their role model, he said, mature beyond her 13 years. Not a eulogy, just the simple truth.

Rabbi Kamin's usually twinkling eyes were sorrowful. His voice breaking, he described Ruth's kindness, her intelligence, and especially her love of children. Ruth babysat for his six children and tutored one of his daughters.

"Six children—how do you take care of six children?" I used to ask her.

"Oh, this one had a friend over, that one was at a friend's house, another was napping, and that only left three to deal with," she would reply with an assurance that I, her mother, couldn't comprehend.

Tears ran in an unending stream down my face while other bearded men in dark suits praised Ruth's character and devotion to Jewish learning.

Later, I trembled under the February sky that pressed down on the cemetery. My father and I held each other up as we watched the coffin lowered.

We waited endlessly, painfully, interminably while people from Ruth's life threw dirt into the grave with the backs of their shovels, a traditional sign of reluctance to say good-bye. Her father. Her brother. Her Uncle Harry. Her cousin Peggy. Her friend Joey. Grim-faced teachers. Crying friends. One put down the spade, and the next took it up. Shovelful by shovelful, thud by thud, each clod crushed me with its finality.

As a Reform Jew, Dad had never witnessed a burial at which the mourners filled in the grave. "This really clops you on the head. It doesn't let you deny that she is gone," he muttered.

All I do is wait, I recall thinking. A lifetime of waiting in the 13 days since the intoxicated driver's car had destroyed Ruth's brain stem and left my effervescent daughter comatose. And now more waiting while the hole in the ground slowly filled. Will it never end? How will I fill my emptiness? How will I keep going?

Barely 24 hours later, our niece, Peggy, accompanied Julian and me to services to welcome the Sabbath. We went to the Orthodox shul where Ruth had led junior congregation.

Fighting the February cold, we climbed the concrete stairs and opened the heavy wooden door. Inside, we hesitated. Several men rushed toward us, encircled Julian, and pulled him into the sanctuary. As if Peggy and I didn't exist.

"Where's the women's section?" Peggy asked.

I pointed. She led me up the narrow staircase, past the low bookshelf of prayer books and Bibles, and along the balcony railing. We climbed a few more steps and sat looking out at the garish chandelier. There may have been a few women downstairs behind the mechitza. The dividing wall was too high for me to see over, but we were the only ones in the balcony.

Below us, I heard a mumble of prayers, loud enough to drown out my snuffling. I half expected Ruth to appear, as she had on those occasional Saturday mornings that I had prayed in this shul. I could almost see her: a slim young teenager with little girls clustered about, eager for her attention, certain of her love. But unlike those Sabbath mornings, tonight the young children sat with their fathers or helped their mothers prepare Shabbat dinner at home. The loving teen was a mirage. Only Peggy's presence saved me from total desolation in my lonely, piercing grief.

Our Cleveland rabbi came to Rochester for the funeral and warned me that I would end up comforting those who came to comfort me. He was right. During shiva, the seven-day mourning period following the funeral, the only people I wanted to talk to, amidst the throngs that filled our living room, were two visitors whom I knew only casually, both mothers of sons who had died as teenagers. How could anyone else understand? I was grateful to the rabbis who came the day after shiva ended to let us know that though the swarms of people had left, we were not alone.

A month later came Purim. I tried to work up some enthusiasm. It was unfair to Miriam to ignore the day totally. But I couldn't get past the fact that Purim had been Ruth's favorite holiday. I pictured her the previous year dressed in her red, one-piece footed pajamas, with "stink-pink" riddles pinned all over on triangular, brightly colored paper. (Question: what's a "stink-pink" for the pageant at which King Ahasuerus selected Esther? Answer: queen scene.) I managed to bake hamentaschen with Miriam, but for years, arranging the platters of goodies, deciding who should receive them, mapping our route, and delivering them had been a mother-daughter activity for the three of us. The mere thought of doing it without Ruth opened the floodgates. How could I drive through a waterfall of tears? How could I handle the interaction? How could I smile in the month that we are commanded to be happy? I just couldn't do it. Fortunately, a friend offered to take Miriam along to deliver our mishloach manot as well as her family's. My community to the rescue, once again.

A few weeks later, a yeshiva rabbi's wife, mother of one of Miriam's classmates, offered to clean "any area of the house you're having trouble getting to" for Passover. This kind woman checked Ruth's bedroom for crumbs, an act that combined her concern for ritual details with profound compassion.

43

Every time Julian passed Ruth's bedroom in those barren days following her death, he closed the door, trying to shut out its painful emptiness. In retrospect, this was a perfect metaphor for his attempt to push away his emotions.

"Only rationality matters," he told me repeatedly, while his stony face and ramrod posture screamed his pain. "Emotions? I have no emotions."

"You're wrong," I insisted. "God created us with both feelings and intellect, with emotions and reason, and to deny either is to deny part of our humanness."

Finding no way to justify a God who would kill three girls who were following Jewish law and tradition at a wholesome convention of Orthodox Jewish youth, Julian turned his back on God, friends, and—without intending or even knowing—family. He even told me, mere months after Ruth died, that he would simply act as if she had never existed.

While he went overboard on intellect, most of the time I was a quivering puddle of emotion. Between crying jags, I found a tiny measure of comfort in wearing Ruth's clothing and jewelry. I ceased riding in cars on the Sabbath both to honor her commitment and to enfold myself in her life. And I opened her bedroom door every time I walked past.

What little peace I found was in connection: with memories, with Larry and Miriam, with Ruth's friends, and with mine. I had always treasured solitude, but now I found it intolerable. Alone, I couldn't control where my thoughts went; people helped distract me and keep me present in the moment.

My first visit to Atlanta after Ruth's death was particularly painful. She should have been there to enjoy the azure sky and vivid flowers. She should have explored the attic and taken home some of my old books. She should have played in the wooded ravine behind the house and skipped rocks in the creek at the bottom. My childhood haunts seemed tainted by her absence.

One day Mom and I set out for a walk. I was pushing Mom's wheelchair down the driveway when she exclaimed, "It should have been me!"

My grief was too raw to disagree, my daughterly devotion too strong to concur. Glad that she couldn't see the tears dripping down my face, I responded shakily, "Mother, we don't have those choices." How I longed for the healthy mother who would have hugged me, held me, and mingled her tears with mine.

Among the many letters we received after Ruth's death—letters I read and reread in the middle of many sleepless nights, Miriam's cat nuzzling my feet—was one from an Atlanta rabbi, with whom I had attended graduate school. "She will be a grand addition to the entourage of noble souls of the pure and righteous who surround God in his heaven," he wrote in words that might have comforted someone with a stronger belief in an afterlife. But I wanted her here, in my house, adding her zest for life to her earthly entourage.

Questions assaulted me. Why Ruth? Why me? Why my family? We're reasonably good people. We don't deserve this.

My Orthodox friends told me that this was God's plan, that we're all "in His pocket." As a religion major and theology student, I was familiar with the age-old problems of good and evil, divine omnipotence vs. human free will. When my sister had died four years earlier, I had even convinced myself that when your time is up, it's up. But this wasn't the sister with whom I had a rocky, if loving, relationship. This was my daughter, the child who had thanked me for naming her "Ruth Leah," the tantrum-throwing child who had metamorphosed into a poised, friendly, smart, and caring young woman. She was the one of whom I used to say, when my girlfriend and I talked about our children during long walks, "I don't worry about Ruth. She has a strong sense of her self and a strong sense of other people; she'll always land on her feet." Of course, I hadn't factored in a drunk driver.

One day Cantor Gartenhaus led me along the streets near my home, walking with me as he had in Utica. "Why?" I asked him. "Why Ruth? Why at an NCSY convention? Why on Shabbat?"

Forsythia, tulips, and jonquils were just starting to color the yards we passed. "It's God's will. God controls everything. We don't understand, but we don't see it from God's point of view."

Inwardly I fumed. Easy answers that were no answers at all.

"And what if we were talking about your Gittie?" I asked. "Would you say the same thing? Would you still be so sure it was God's will?"

"Oh yes," he assured me. But I didn't believe him.

I called Rabbi Harris, head of the yeshiva and father of Miriam's best friend, and said I'd like to ask him some questions. He came by the next day. He lowered his tall, slender frame onto the sofa. I sat nearby on my favorite chair.

"Why? Why Ruth? Why when she was following the Torah? Why?"

"Even though we can't understand," he said, "we know it is God's will because God controls the universe."

"And what if we were talking about your Fagie? Would you say the same thing? Would you still be so sure it was God's will?"

He looked down at his hands. I stared past him at the afghan that Ruth had crocheted to match our family room décor. After a long pause, head still down, he said, "I don't know. I hope so."

Another time I approached Rabbi Kamin, Larry's favorite yeshiva rabbi. Ruth babysat for his children and tutored his daughter, Deena. "Why?" I asked. "Why Ruth? Why?"

"Maybe in the world to come we'll get answers," he said, "but for now we have to accept that even though we don't always understand, everything that happens is according to God's plan."

"And what if we were talking about your Deena? Would you still be so sure?"

He fiddled with a button on his black coat and looked away. Forced by my anguished question to drop his rabbinic stance and view the question as a father, he, like Rabbi Harris, had to admit that he had no answer.

I was surprised when my close friend, Esther, Rabbi Harris' wife, a pious woman strictly observant of all Jewish laws, said, "Of course I question God. How can a thinking person not raise questions? The difference is that I never stop following the mitzvot, even when I question." I pondered this and continued questioning.

44

"Let all who are hungry come and eat," reads the leader, a chavurah member. But I know that no food will ever fill my hollowness. I turn the Hagaddah's pages on cue, but I am far away, in another time zone. I picture petite, shiny-eyed Ruth asking the four questions, and I cry. I remember the year she knocked on the door and entered with her hobo stick as a wandering Jew, headed toward Jerusalem. My tears could overflow the Nile when I think that she will

never visit the promised land. I spoon some charoset onto my plate and stare at the mixture of apples, nuts, cinnamon, and wine. Last year Ruth prepared it. I'll choke if I try to swallow. Bless God for creating the fruit of the vine? When Ruth's not here? I don't think so. Sing psalms? Praise God? I'm sorry that I'm ruining everyone else's seder, but I can't hide my pain. I'm not sure I want to.

After we sing "Next Year in Jerusalem," I grab Julian, Larry, and Miriam and head for the door, mumbling my thanks and apologies. There's no way I can stay for "Who Knows One."

* * *

One weekend that spring, Temple Beth El hosted a rabbi as a scholar-in-residence. The rabbi led an alternative service that focused on congregational participation and affirmation of God's presence and immediacy. He recited a psalm, and we followed each line with the words, *"Ki l'olam hasdo"* "for His mercy endures forever." Sometimes we said it together, sometimes the men, sometimes the women, sometimes people of different ages. According to the rabbi's instructions we shouted or whispered, always emphasizing God's eternal goodness.

That night we went to a follow-up program. The rabbi spoke, then opened the floor to questions. With a deep breath, telling myself that I could do this without breaking down, I raised my hand. "Sometimes," I said to him, "life slaps you in the face." I barely got the next words out. "In my case, it was my daughter's death by a drunk driver. But whatever it is, how do you keep saying '*ki l'olam hasdo*'?"

Julian shot me a dagger-like look and later rebuked me for subjecting everyone else to my raw anguish.

The rabbi stepped back as if I had struck him. After a long, painful pause, he responded. "What good does it do not to say it?"

His words dumbfounded me. I've thought about them often since then. Because God's existence is independent of my praise, or even my belief, to refuse to say *"ki l'olam hasdo"* doesn't hurt God. Rather, it separates me from the Divine and from my people. If there was anything I wanted in those achingly lonely years after Ruth's death, it was connection. Especially connection with Ruth. I wrapped myself in her life, carrying on for her, doing what she had done. In a wrenching reversal of the natural order, I walked in my child's footsteps until eventually they became my own. Walking, not driving, on Shabbat, for example, became central to my religious and general well-being. And I kept attending services, uttering God's praises, even when I choked over the words. I found I was still climbing the ladder, though teetering on every rung.

As I stumbled through my days, friends took me to lunch, called often, helped to fill endless empty hours. It must not have been easy because Ruth was the only topic I found worth discussing. A lifelong chatterbox, I now had no interest in idle conversation. My desire to speak had died with my child. At the cleaner's, the grocery store, the gas station, I was astonished that people spoke to me in normal tones. Couldn't they see my scarlet B for Bereaved Mother? Didn't they know I was stained by grief? That my child was dead? I was, I thought, the ultimate outsider.

Granny died two months after Ruth. For years, I had wondered how I would react when she left this earth. I knew I would not be as bereft as I had when my Atlanta grandparents had passed away during my childhood. I expected to feel some sadness but mostly gratitude to have had an adult relationship with her. I certainly never expected to be so numb from my daughter's death that Granny's was almost irrelevant. The tiny piece of my consciousness that registered the news thought that maybe my 103-year-old grandmother, fearful of dying, needed her bold great-granddaughter to guide her through whatever came next.

A driver makes countless decisions about when it's safe to cut across traffic. Many a time, as days "since Utica" extended into weeks and months, I was tempted to turn too soon, to set myself up for a crash. The only thing that stopped me was the fear that I would botch it and end up paralyzed like my mother rather than with Ruth, wherever she was.

That spring, Larry muddled through his final semester at the yeshiva. He spent hours on the phone with an NCSY advisor several years his senior, time when he might have been hanging out with Ruth. I hoped that this older friend gave him the consolation and grounding he needed; I was too depressed to do much for him on my own. I did wonder from time to time if the scene he had described to us back in Utica—bodies flying, seeing his sister's face when he leaned down to cover a girl with his jacket—still played in his head. It must have; I kept picturing it, and I had only heard it second-hand. But I was too fearful of reawakening a dormant memory to ask him. Perhaps if I had asked, perhaps if I had insisted on psychotherapy, I could have saved him years of agony, but I was too numb, too mired in my own anguish to be able to reach out.

45

The summer after Ruth's death, Miriam and I accompanied Julian to an academic conference in Madison, Wisconsin. It was a chance to visit Milwaukee, the city where Ruth and Miriam were born and that we had left a decade before. Our pain traveled with us, especially when we reconnected with friends who remembered Ruthie as a toddler. Jane and Marv Klitsner held us tightly. Through my inevitable tears, I saw us all smiling in some earlier, happier life. I remembered Jane's calming voice when I despaired of my young tantrum thrower. I pictured four-year-old Ruthie playing under their dining room table at our last Milwaukee seder.

On Shabbat afternoon, we dropped in on Rabbi Twerski, whose daughter had been in Larry's Hillel Academy class. Julian and Larry sometimes drove to services at his Hasidic congregation, then walked to his home for Shabbat lunch, while I stayed home with my baby daughters.

Julian told him about Ruth. He gasped, looked down, looked back at us. "I read about the Utica incident," he said, "but there were no names. I had no idea that it was your Ruthie." Among the toys scattered on his living room floor, he spotted a yellow pencil—forbidden to be used or even touched on Shabbat—and kicked it under the couch, out of reach of his young children playing nearby. I had barely noticed the little ones, but now I pictured Ruthie at that age and wept.

He continued, "We can't understand God's ways. We can only trust in His ultimate goodness." As usual, this attempt at comfort failed to stem my silent tears.

While Julian was at his Madison meetings, Miriam and I made a two-day jaunt to Chicago. I wondered what we could talk about in the car. She seemed too young to be the kind of companion that Ruth had grown to be. I dreaded silence—and the negative directions my unengaged mind inevitably took. To my relief, Miriam chattered about Colleen Moore's Fairy Castle at the Museum of Science and Industry. She bounced in her seat with excitement to see the display she had read about. I, in turn, told her about the miniature rooms I knew she would enjoy at the Art Institute.

"Each room represents a particular time and style," I explained. "Every piece of furniture and every lamp and candlestick was built to scale by a master craftsman. Maybe you'll get some ideas for your dollhouse."

At the Art Institute, Miriam stood on her tiptoes to peer over a handrail into the tiny dioramas. "Everything is so real!" she exclaimed. "Ooh, I'd love a chandelier like that for my living room."

Her enthusiasm was contagious. "Maybe we can find you one at the miniature shop. Or maybe you and Daddy can make one."

As we sauntered from one miniscule exhibit to the next, I asked, "Do you see anything familiar?"

She scanned the next diorama carefully before pointing to an 18th century French armchair. "That looks like Grandmommy's." A few minutes later she said of a 1930s English drawing room, "I don't like this one. The furniture's too plain."

When did my little girl become so grown up, with her own taste and opinions that she shared like a miniature adult?

Later, at the Museum of Science and Industry, we passed an exhibit of hatching eggs on our way to Colleen Moore's Fairy Castle. Only the delight of watching fuzzy chicks poke through their shells could compete with the castle's enchantment. Driving back to Madison, we talked about what we'd seen. There were none of the heavy silences that I'd dreaded. No awkward thrashing around for words to fill a disquieting vacuum. I discovered that my eleven-year-old "baby" could, indeed, be a companion able to converse interestingly about her interests and perspectives. Perhaps she could help fill my hollowness. Her sunny nature helped pull me toward the future.

46

Plans for Larry's post-high school year in Israel had vanished into a fog of despair and loss. Neither he nor we could bear the thought of his being so far away. Instead, he enrolled at Yeshiva University. The six-hour drive to New York City to deposit him at the dorm seemed endless. A year before, we'd have gabbed about his upcoming freshman year, if he'd like his roommate, when he'd next be home. I'd have said something trite about parents giving their children roots and wings. I'd have been excited with and for him. But now, barely half a year after his sister's death, words seemed futile. I was terrified that something horrible would happen to him in the big city. The pain of departure draped the long ride in silence.

Back home, I discovered I hadn't used up all my tears. I had always enjoyed being alone, but now I found solitude to be intolerable. Day after day, I called a friend, cried and talked about Ruth for half an hour, hung up and immediately dialed another. Some friends took me to lunch, others for long walks. Somehow the days dragged by. In six months, our household had dropped from five to three. Not buying Ruth's favorite foods made grocery shopping painful, dinnertime seemed bleak, and the absences—especially THE absence—governed our existence. Despite our best intentions, Julian and I grew more distant as we each struggled to find our own way to cope.

Meanwhile, people sought ways to honor and memorialize Ruth's short, packed life. Julian spent hours of the next year working with a member of the synagogue where Ruth had led groups to transform a seldom-used room into a children's library. The afternoon Hebrew school our daughter had attended for just one semester offered an award to the outstanding eighth grade Hebrew student—given posthumously to Ruth the first year and, three years later, to Miriam. The public school Ruth had attended for that same semester presented a writing award in her name. I found these tributes bittersweet. On the one hand, it was gratifying that Ruth had affected so many lives. On the other, she should still be sharing her brand of friendship, intelligence, and élan; if she had made such a difference in not quite fourteen years, imagine what she could have done in eighty-four.

When our insurance agent called to ask how to disburse an insurance policy on Ruth's life, we directed the proceeds to Ruth's beloved Camp Ramah. The camp built an outdoor stage overlooking the lake. We attended the dedication the next summer. One of her friends told us that this had been her favorite spot in the camp she adored. We watched campers dance to the songs they said were her favorites. One included the words, "I haven't loved enough" and the other, from *Pirkei Avot*, "It's not for you to finish the task...." The irony, the setting, seeing Ruth's friends, remembering Ruth in a visitor's day performance the year before... my tears could have turned that lovely Canadian lake into a saltwater sea.

Although Julian and I were together that day at Camp Ramah, we were each isolated in our own grief. Not wanting to add to each other's burden, we each kept our thoughts to ourselves, unwittingly intensifying our separate pain.

47

Before the High Holidays, we switched our membership from Temple Beth El, site of Ruth's bat mitzvah, back to Congregation Beth Sholom, where we had celebrated Larry's bar mitzvah. This was not so much a carefully researched and planned decision as it was a move based on a jumble of emotional reactions: The Beth El memories were too painful, we preferred the Beth Sholom rabbi's warmth to the Beth El rabbi's aloofness, and the Orthodox community had embraced us with outstretched arms.

Filled with Ruth's absence, the holy days were bound to be difficult, no matter where we worshipped. "May you be written in the Book of Life," we had greeted each other the previous Rosh Hashanah. I had long found this metaphor troubling. The Book of Life seemed too much like Santa's checklist, with the "nice" surviving another year and the names of the "naughty" stricken out forever.

Particularly disturbing was a prayer recited on both Rosh Hashanah and Yom Kippur: "On New Year's Day the decree is inscribed and on the Day of Atonement it is sealed, how many shall pass away and how many shall be born; who shall live and who shall die;...who shall perish by fire and who by water; who by earthquake and who by plague...." Who by a driver's drunken indifference to life... Had Ruth's February death been decreed at this time last year? "But repentance, prayer, and righteousness avert the evil decree," concludes the prayer. Hadn't we prayed hard enough? Given enough to charity? Atoned for our misdeeds? Could we, or I, have somehow warded off Ruth's death?

But my high holiday prayers in 1981 were less about my sins, how I might change, than about whether or not there was a God who cared what I did. I recalled my friend Esther's words—it's all right to question as long as you keep doing the mitzvot—and, as I had every year that I could remember, I fasted and went to services. But mostly I turned pages, cried, and questioned.

Each Yom Kippur, as darkness falls and the service reaches its conclusion, the cantor, followed by the congregation, pronounces the "Sh'ma," "Hear, O Israel, the Lord is our God, the Lord is one." Then three times the cantor, followed by the congregation, recites in Hebrew, "Blessed be the Name whose glorious kingdom is for ever and ever." Finally, the cantor and congregation end with the sevenfold recitation of three Hebrew words, "The Lord He is God," in a crescendo that ends with a long shofar blast. Relief, fatigue, and hunger mingle as the day of fasting and prayer ends.

But that year, Cantor Gartenhaus's voice took me away from the congregation, back to the Utica hospital room where he had stood at Ruth's bedside and sung to her. I stood numb, sad, weepy. *"Sh'ma Yisrael..."* The words seemed to come from far away. *"Baruch Shem Cavod," "Blessed be the Name..."* Unable to utter a word, I simply stood with tears falling.

"The Lord, He is God." In Hebrew, the cantor echoed the prophet Elijah's triumphant proclamation of God's unity and essential righteousness.

He repeated, louder, *"Adonai, Hu HaElohim."*

Louder still: *"HaShem, Hu HaElohim."*

By now he was shouting. *"HaShem, Hu HaElohim."*

"HaShem, Hu HaElohim." He pounded his fist.

"HaShem, Hu HaElohim," he roared.

And with a final, slow bellow, *"HaShem, Hu HaElohim."*

The congregation repeated the words, then broke into Kaddish, a prayer that praises God. The blast of the ram's horn felt anti-climactic. I was still wrapped in Cantor Gartenhaus's voice, which seemed to convey my anguish, and his, to the furthest corners of the universe. As if to protest Ruth's death. As if to demand an explanation. As if to convince us both that God exists.

In Hebrew, the one who leads prayers is called shaliach tzibur, the community's messenger. As my emissary that Yom Kippur, the cantor carried fury, sorrow, and despair straight from my heart to the heavens.

48

I probably helped Julian erect our sukkah for the holiday that followed five days later. I most likely served meals in it and dragged myself to services. But my only clear memory is refusing to go to services for the Simhat Torah celebration. During the evening's festivities people circle the Torah in joyous dance. Ruth's second grade teacher, an Israeli dance expert, had taught her students simplified versions of many steps. At Camp Ramah, Ruth had participated in Israeli dance performances. She and Israeli dancing were too firmly connected in my mind for me to even watch, much less participate. Julian took Miriam to services, but I stayed home and wept. I couldn't imagine that I would ever again rejoice—in the Torah or anything else.

On the one hand, emulating Ruth's observance of Shabbat and holidays comforted me. On the other, participating in activities that she had loved intensified the phantom pain of my amputated heart.

Within a year or two of Ruth's death, I read Rabbi Harold Kushner's newly published book, *When Bad Things Happen to Good People*. His son had died a few years before at the same age as Ruth. Unlike Ruth, who had led a blessed life, Kushner's son had suffered many years from progeria, rapid aging. Kushner describes the theological problem that arises from the tension between the ideas of an omnipotent God, a just God, and the bad things that often happen to good people. He rejects the notion, expressed most eloquently by the three visitors who tried to comfort Job, that a just, all-powerful God causes suffering as punishment for misdeeds. Instead, Kushner claims that God, acting from divine omnipotence, chose to give up some power in order to create humans with free will. God doesn't choose to cause pain and suffering. Sometimes it results from nature-set-in-motion. Other times, people acting freely do bad things like drive after drinking for six hours. When bad things happen, God, the good, compassionate, less-powerful-by-his-own-choice God, cries with you.

Kushner's book resonated with me, and I urged Julian to read it.

"This presents theological underpinnings to positions I've arrived at intuitively," I told him. "It's not God who killed Ruth, it's the drunk driver."

Julian disagreed. "If God made the heavens and the earth and everything in it, if he's omnipotent and omnipresent, then he could have prevented this."

I defended Kushner's position. "The title isn't 'Why Bad Things Happen to Good People.' It's '*When* Bad Things Happen.' It's showing me how I can reach toward God now, when I need him."

But Julian wasn't about to let God off the hook. The God he rejected had to follow the rules of strict Orthodoxy, rules that Julian himself turned his back on. I, on the other hand, found that Kushner's views enabled me to pray that God help me now. Kushner's description of the purposes of prayer made sense to me: to connect to God and to people who share my concerns, and to help me "tap hidden reserves of faith and courage which were not available to me before." Heaven knew, I needed every ounce of faith and courage I could summon just to get out of bed and stumble through the day.

The next time Larry was home on vacation from college, I described Kushner's theology. Larry was taking a course in Jewish philosophy.

"That's not so radical. One of the rabbis we studied this semester said almost the same thing."

I wondered if this rabbi, too, wrote from personal pain rather than from abstract philosophical musing.

At some point during Larry's college years, he suggested a different reading of the high holidays prayer that had continued to trouble me: "On New Year's Day the decree is inscribed and on the Day of Atonement it is sealed ... who shall live and who shall die...But repentance, prayer, and righteousness avert the evil decree." Most English translations make the word "evil" an adjective, but in Hebrew it is a noun. It is truer to the Hebrew though more awkward in English to read the verse, "Repentance, prayer, and righteousness avert the evil *of* the decree."

My actions can help ward off not the fact but the evil *effect* of the decree. This interpretation has allowed me to read the words with less turmoil. I will always see Ruth's young death as a despicable, unforgivable crime against the entire universe, but I can choose, to some extent, how I let it affect me. I can let my Jewish tradition and kindness, rather than malevolence, govern my life.

One Sabbath evening, several years after Ruth's death, I struck a match, then carefully lit five candles, one for each member of my family. I circled the flames three times with my hands to draw the holiness of Shabbat into my home and my soul, then brought them to my face to cover my eyes. "*Baruch atah*, blessed are You…." As I said the blessing, eyes closed, I sensed a candle shoot upward, sputtering to call attention to itself. Only the candle's hiccoughing hisses broke the Sabbath stillness. I was sure that it was Ruth, calling to me, telling me she was okay, that she was with me at this moment that marked the separation between ordinary time and the weekly taste of eternity.

49

Starting with the year we had moved to Cleveland, we had spent Thanksgiving with my family, alternating between our home and New

Jersey, where my sisters lived. The yeshiva Larry attended for high school held classes on Thanksgiving Day. I never let him go to school on Thanksgiving, even on the years when we feasted in Rochester, because I considered it important for him to celebrate the quintessential American holiday. This was the day I could feel fully American, fully Jewish, while enjoying an infrequent visit with extended family. When a Jewish school holds classes on Christmas day, I have no complaint; it's a Christian holiday. Discourage Jewish children from trick and treat activities? Halloween's Christian roots and present-day focus on magic and superstition make it understandable, though I personally had no objection to my kids' participation. But boycott Thanksgiving? Outrageous! This is the day that pays tribute to the survival of a band of people who fled religious persecution (how Jewish is that?) and echoes their gratitude to the Almighty. After the first year or two at the yeshiva, Larry gave up the fight. He knew that he would spend the holiday with us, whether in Rochester or in New Jersey.

In honor of the holiday's religious roots, we had developed a tradition of giving everyone at the table the opportunity to express gratitude.

"I'm thankful for my good health and family."

"I'm grateful to be here with my aunt and uncle and cousins."

"I'm thankful for my Legos."

"I'm thankful for my friends and that my teachers are nice this year."

"Thank you for mommy and daddy and teddy bear."

Julian and I hosted Thanksgiving 1981. Mid-afternoon, when the turkey's savory aroma filled the house, I called everyone to dinner. At the table, the children waited expectantly for Julian to lead off with "I'm thankful for." Instead, after a long pause, he reached for Margaret's plate. "Dark meat or light?"

I sighed in relief. People reached for the serving dishes.

"Let's pass everything in one direction." Margaret took some squash pudding and started it clockwise around the table.

By unspoken agreement, we had skipped the verbal first course. The enormity of our loss flavored our feast with melancholy.

50

"Mazel tov, mazel tov."

"Miriam, how pretty you look!"

Miriam's always-rosy cheeks brightened with pleasure. She wore a new dress; her hair gleamed. It was a March Shabbat in 1982, ten days after she had turned twelve on the Hebrew calendar. At the Orthodox synagogue to which we now belonged, girls celebrate their acceptance of the commandments at twelve rather than thirteen. It was barely a year after Ruth's death, and planning a grocery list, or even what to serve for dinner, overwhelmed me. How could I have planned a major event?

Our chavurah came to the rescue. One member taught Miriam to lead services. Another offered her home. We invited a few extra friends and called it a "mini-bat."

"Do you know Nancy and Howard? Barbara and Ron?" We introduced our friends to the chavurah regulars. Soon everyone had gathered on the folding chairs lined up in the living room.

We always began our service with a short prayer, selected by a member of the group, to help set the mood. I stepped forward, took a deep breath—no tears today, right?—and began.

"Welcome to Miriam's bat mitzvah. We are so pleased to be surrounded by our closest friends as we mark this special time in her life." Another deep breath to steady my voice. I had often delivered the opening prayer and frequently turned to our Cleveland rabbi's book, *The Fire Waits.* His approach to this week's Torah portion was a perfect tie-in to Miriam's bat mitzvah.

On the High Priest's forehead,
Carved on gold,
Hung these words:
"Holy to the Lord."
Look at the forehead
Of every man.
Can you see the words?

Can you make them out?
"Holy to the Lord."
...
Is that lipstick straight?
Or, do you need a shave?
Look again and see the writing

On your face:
"Holy to the Lord."

I put the book down. "Miriam, you are a loving, wonderful daughter. Someday you will care that your lipstick is on straight, but your words and deeds have already shown, and I know will continue to demonstrate, that being 'Holy to the Lord' is inscribed on your heart."

A friend led the morning service, then Julian rose to give a *d'var Torah* that compared Miriam to Bezalel, the artist in charge of building the Tabernacle. The Bible refers to Bezalel as *chacham lev,* wise of heart. "Miriam, you have the love of art, and the warmth of feeling ... to create both physical and spiritual beauty ... I hope you will be able to grow in the wisdom of your heart, in your depth of feelings, and you will be granted the way to share your sense of beauty and caring with others."

Miriam led our tiny congregation through the remainder of the service. Though I knew she was nervous, she appeared calm. This was the payoff for all those years of day school tuition. She was comfortable with the Hebrew and understood and believed the prayers. Ruth would have been so proud of her sister, I thought.

Afterward, we served a buffet luncheon. For Julian and me, this was a perfect celebration: small, warm, focused on the child and the service, without embellishment. Not surprisingly, Miriam saw it differently.

"Larry and Ruth had big parties. I want one, too!"

"But Miriam, you had a lovely celebration."

"My grandparents weren't here. Aunt Margaret and Aunt Shirley weren't here. Neither were my other aunts and uncles and cousins. And those were your friends, not mine."

How could we deny her the excitement, the drama, the presents that we would have taken for granted… before?

Barely a year after Ruth's death, I began planning a second bat mitzvah for Miriam, this one at Beth Sholom. My goal was to make it as unlike Ruth's as possible: different synagogue, seated luncheon rather than outdoor buffet, singalong with slides rather than Israeli dancing. Miriam's goal was to do as much as an Orthodox rabbi would allow. Our rabbi was still experimenting with how best to acknowledge a girl's coming of age, learning, and commitment within the constraints imposed by Orthodoxy: no female could be called to the Torah for an aliyah, no female could lead services. We settled on a Sunday morning ceremony, not a service.

We all missed Julian's father, who had fallen ill not long after his granddaughter's death and been moved into Atlanta's Jewish Home. Miriam's other three grandparents, most of her aunts and uncles, and her closest cousins joined us on Labor Day weekend, along with several out-of-town friends. The southerners, in particular, enjoyed Shabbat afternoon in our backyard, the sunny, crisp day a welcome change from Atlanta's late summer humidity.

By now Dad was accustomed to our Shabbat rituals and sat with good grace through Friday night kiddush and Saturday night's havdalah ceremony that separated Shabbat from the six weekdays to come. Only the awkward perch of a gold satin kipa on his balding head at the Sunday morning ceremony revealed his discomfort at being in Orthodox surroundings. Like all of us, he carried deep pain about Ruth's death, but throughout Mom's illness he had shown me how to carry on in the face of loss and despair. This weekend was no different: He was gentle and solicitous with Mom, proud of Miriam, and loving with us all.

On Sunday morning, Miriam stood on the bima—the altar—her dressy brown outfit complementing her light brown hair. She led the congregation in a responsive reading. Then, looking at a Hebrew Bible, not the Torah scroll, she chanted the song of Moses that describes crossing the Red Sea and ends with these lines:

"And Miriam the prophetess, Aaron's sister, took a timbrel in her hand; and all the women went after her in dance with timbrels. And Miriam chanted for them:

Sing to the Lord, for He has triumphed gloriously;
Horse and driver He has hurled into the sea."

With a relieved grin, she launched into her *d'var Torah.* "The reason I chose this passage is because it mentions Miriam. My parents named me after the biblical Miriam, not after a relative, though if I had been a boy I would have been named after my great-uncle Herman Heyman."

Dad turned to me. "Really? You never told me that." I could tell he was moved and honored that we had considered naming our baby for his brother, who had died 10 months before Miriam's birth.

Miriam continued. "My bat mitzvah seems like a good time to learn about the biblical Miriam and decide if she is a proper role model to follow as I try to decide what type of life I want to lead." Her clear blue eyes shone under the sanctuary lights. "Miriam teaches me to praise God for what he does for me. To be joyful, happy, and enthusiastic so others will want to follow me...."

I hope she will have a long, happy life, I thought. Her joy and enthusiasm seemed to be all that could penetrate my sorrow.

"Why does the passage say 'sister of Aaron,' not sister of Moses, or daughter of Amram?" she asked. As she enumerated reasons cited by the rabbis, I thought how ironic that Miriam spoke about a woman best known as someone's sister, when her own sister's absence hovered over us all.

Like her brother and sister before her, Miriam impressed me with her assurance, poise, and commitment to Judaism. Though she was only entering seventh grade, her Hebrew was far more fluent than my bumbling efforts. Despite my master's degree in biblical studies, her knowledge of Jewish commentators surpassed mine. I admired, and even envied, the faith that she and her brother seemed to have caught from their Jewish teachers and classmates. At least Julian and I could take some credit, I thought, for their strong sense of right and wrong... and for sending them to Jewish day schools.

Miriam's bat mitzvah at Beth Sholom:
Julian, B.J., Miriam, Mom, Larry, Dad

51

Gradually, one minute at a time, one foot in front of the other, our lives took on some semblance of normalcy. We all struggled, sometimes together, sometimes separately. Counseling helped. Friends helped. A support group, the Compassionate Friends, helped. I remember smiling wryly when an acquaintance said, "Such a tragedy must bring you and Julian so much closer together." But different styles in grieving chipped at our relationship and added to our suffering. Judaism, which had always bound us together, now divided us. As I moved toward more tradition, in part as a way to feel close to Ruth, he shunned the religion that he blamed for her death. Already feeling like a statistic as mother of one of that year's 25,000 victims of intoxicated driving, I was determined not to be among the 70 percent of bereaved parents who divorce. That statistic in Harriet Schiff's *The Bereaved Parent* strengthened my will to hang on to my marriage, no matter how difficult.

Almost immediately after Ruth's death, someone had taken Julian and me to a meeting of Rochester Against Intoxicated Driving. The crash that had killed three young pedestrians attending a youth group convention had been in the public eye for the twelve days that Ruth lay comatose. The media had been told that we would attend the meeting, and the TV cameras came out in force. While I sat in the corner, in a fetal position, tears staining my face, Julian spoke about the horrifying effects of intoxicated driving and the need for community action. How he had the presence and eloquence was beyond me.

Bit by bit, I became active in the organization. Soon after Ruth's death, an older youth group friend of hers had asked if I would speak to her high school health science class. I agreed. That gave me an excuse to pore over notebooks of slides Julian had taken of the children. A photographer friend helped me select pictures that depicted Ruth's life. The health teacher and students found my presentation meaningful, and I was invited back every semester until the teacher retired. At some point, I wrote a script (I'm still surprised my tears didn't short out the keyboard) so that others could show "The Story of Ruth." Soon, chapters of RAID's national affiliate were using it around the country, and I also continued to present it to various Rochester school and community groups. Every time the clouds depicting Ruth's coma appeared on the screen and I heard the catch in my recorded voice, my heart started thumping. This time—and I reacted this way, over and over, for years—the story was going to turn out differently. This time the clouds would give way to sunshine. Ruth would make a full recovery.

One day I received a call from the president of Remove Intoxicated Drivers, RAID's national group. "I have wonderful news," she began.

Ruth is coming home flashed through my head.

But no, of course not. The "wonderful news" was that photos of Ruth and other victims had encouraged the New York State Legislature to pass stronger anti-DWI laws. Ruth was continuing to make a difference, both through these laws and through the slideshow's effect, but she wasn't coming home again. Ever.

One afternoon a teenager approached me in a parking lot. "You're the lady who showed us the slides about Ruth, aren't you? Well, you ruined my day. By the time Ruth died, I felt as if I had lost a close friend."

Goal achieved. I hoped this meant that she, and the hundreds of others who viewed "The Story of Ruth" through the years, would never drive after drinking, would stay out of cars with drunken drivers, and would support strong laws. I'll never know if I saved any lives, but this was work I felt compelled to do, no matter how difficult. My parents had modeled the importance of community service. Judaism demands social action. And it says in the Talmud (Tractate Sanhedrin 4:8) that "He who saves a single life, is considered as if he had saved the entire world." Perhaps I could preserve another family's universe.

Even when I had come out of the worst of my depression, my pain—and unending tears—continued, and Miriam did her best to comfort me. I hated the burden my melancholy placed on her. Besides, she had her own grief to deal with. One evening she dropped her head on my chest and wailed, "Everybody else knew her better than I did."

Our Shabbat morning walks to synagogue gave us time to talk about what bothered her most, her unresolved sibling rivalry with Ruth.

"You would have become good friends someday," I assured her. "You just needed a few more years.

"You and Aunt Leslie never did."

"True, but I'm positive you and Ruth would have. You'll just have to take my word for it." My words were sincere, but I knew Miriam didn't believe them.

"When I meet Ruth in *olam ha-ba,* the world to come, first I'm going to punch her in the nose, 'cause finally I'll be stronger than she is, and then I'm going to tell her I love her."

How sad, I thought, to be left feeling that you never really knew your sister, and had never admitted to yourself, much less to her, that you loved her.

I no longer enjoyed my own morose company. I found it nearly impossible, when alone, to prevent the downward spiral of questions: Why Ruth? Why us? Why me? Why? Why? Why? From my window, I often saw a blue-jacketed student walking home from school and expected Ruth to burst through the door. Day after day, disappointment struck my heart. I knew I had to get out of the house, find a job, be with people.

I bought a job search manual, followed it explicitly, and became the first director of development for a private school for learning disabled teenagers. The position gave me the opportunity to be around students the same age that Ruth would have been. The nurturing environment was just what I needed. And the work enabled me to identify with thirteen-year-old Ruth's stated career goal of teaching "handicapped children, because normal children would be too boring."

Like her siblings before her, Miriam left Hillel School at the end of 7th grade to enter Twelve Corners Middle School. Ruth's NCSY friends adopted Miriam, and the youth group became the center of her social life. I shuddered at the thought of the National Conference of Synagogue Youth; Ruth had died at an NCSY convention. But Miriam found her place in the organization, and it was good for her. It strengthened her Jewish identity, knowledge, and observance. More importantly, it was a measure of stability in a life turned upside down.

As she moved from middle to high school, she was elected to NCSY offices. She became national chairman of the youth group's outreach program to young Jews with hearing loss and then, in her senior year, president of the upstate New York region. Sending her off to conventions was incredibly painful, even though participants now were required to wear neon orange vests when walking at night … after the figurative horse was out of the barn. I gritted my teeth, smiled shakily, gave her a hug, and tried to hide my feelings.

At Shabbat services, when the Torah is returned to the ark, the congregation sings in Hebrew, "[The Torah] is a tree of life to them that hold fast to it, and all who uphold it are happy. Its ways are ways of pleasantness and all its paths are peace." Whenever the cantor used the plaintive tune he had chanted at Ruth's bedside, I felt myself right back in her hospital room. I would remove my glasses and feel the drops trickle down my face. If Miriam were there, she would hug me. Sometimes a friend would notice and pat my shoulder. Other times, I sobbed silently, alone with my thoughts and memories. Ruth died because she held fast to Torah, because she walked on Shabbat. While I hadn't given up totally on Torah, I doubted that I would ever again be happy or at peace.

One day I found myself entreating, with the concluding line of the prayer, "Turn us unto You, O Lord, and we shall return; renew our days as of old." Please, God, whoever you are, if you can't turn back the days to a time before Utica, when I had Ruth at my side, then help me to feel like myself again. Help me see beauty, as Ruth saw beauty. Help me care about people, as Ruth cared about people. Help me regain a sense of myself, as Ruth had a strong sense of self. Help me carry on for Ruth.

52

Despite my desire to pull myself out of depression, challenges arose daily in the simplest things. Trying not to burst into tears when I saw Ruth's friends. Stamping "Yudelson" on Miriam's camp clothes and not on Ruth's. Encountering her favorite (or least favorite) food, or book, or movie. And surviving February. For some long forgotten reason, I opened the *World Book* to read about calendars, and discovered that the Romans skipped the month of February. Brilliant, I thought. Why can't I just skip that miserable month? Ruth was struck on the 6th, died on the 18th, and didn't turn fourteen on the 25th. Little girls from the Utica Hebrew School had brought Valentines to Ruth in the hospital, so even that seemingly benign day became sorrowful. And then there were the parallel Hebrew dates that fluctuated between February and March. Eventually, over the course of years or maybe decades, I progressed from stumbling from one horrible marker to another throughout the month to releasing my sorrow with one good cry on one of those occasions.

One summer Larry visited his grandparents in Atlanta alone. Always before, I had been there to purchase kosher food and oversee its preparation. I had figured out how to observe a semblance of Shabbat in the midst of a Saturday-weekend environment. But this time it was up to Larry, zealous in his observance, to make his Jewish practices work within his grandparents' secular household. This was not only his first visit without me to run interference; it was his first trip to Atlanta without Ruth as his companion. We underestimated the challenges.

With Mom an invalid, Dad was household manager. He cooperated in the sense that he insisted on reimbursing us for whatever kosher food we bought. But he neither understood nor sympathized. He certainly did not understand when Larry refused to join his grandparents at dinner on Friday evening. My parents had gotten in the habit of dining at 5:30 in order to let the cook go home at a reasonable time. Larry could have chosen to eat with them, hours before sunset, then light candles, chant kiddush over a glass of wine, and eat a light meal at the appointed hour. Or he could have kept them company while they ate. He might have reached another compromise, such as offering to do the clean-up if they ate later. Instead, he closeted himself in his bedroom to follow his own schedule and the letter of the law as he understood it. By the time he emerged close to sundown, somewhere between 8 and 9, darkness had fallen on his grandparents as well. He had offended them deeply.

My father, who valued truth as much as family, let me know about Larry's breach of good sense and manners. "If this is what your observance does...."

"No, Dad." I hoped my voice would be steady as it traveled over the telephone wires. "Larry is young, he's literal, and he's hurting emotionally."

Inwardly, I agreed with Dad. Larry could have found a way to honor both his grandparents and Shabbat. One of my friends had once asked Larry, "If you spend all your time following the commandments, what room is there for you to exercise your free will?"

Larry's answer had impressed me, "I have to choose how much time I spend on which mitzvah." He had made a poor choice in Atlanta, but

I knew he would make better ones in the future. His was a questioning mind, and he already juggled devotion to tradition and law with intellectual openness to twentieth century knowledge. A different friend had asked him how he reconciled his interest in science with the biblical account of creation.

"And if you were God, describing creation to a bunch of primitive people, how would you explain it?" He was willing to view the creation story metaphorically. His fascination with science protected him from the close-mindedness of a literal, fundamentalist reading of the Bible. But after the Atlanta trip, I worried about what seemed to me to be a blind adherence to *halachah*, Jewish law, at the expense of sensitivity to the people he loved. Perhaps his grief and loneliness limited his ability to think of a better way to meet both their needs and his.

Over the next few years, Dad framed his concern as a conflict between the fourth commandment, "Remember the Sabbath day to keep it holy," and the fifth, "Honor your father and your mother." He viewed Larry's actions as exalting the ritual over the ethical injunctions. Had Larry really honored God when he dishonored his grandparents in the process? For Dad, Jewish ritual was irrelevant to a good life. Treating others with respect and integrity was, on the other hand, the deeply ingrained foundation of his existence. This presumed dichotomy was the source of his deathbed question to me fifteen or so years later. I understood the question behind the question: Which will take precedence, your devotion to Shabbat ritual and strictures or your love and respect for me?

53

On a Shabbat morning in early January 1985, four years after Ruth's death, I sat in my usual seat at Beth Sholom. The rabbi's sermon about Joseph being sold into slavery floated through the air. My headed nodded, and I jerked myself upright. What is it about this rabbi's voice that always puts me to sleep? I asked myself.

"There is a Jewish imperative to redeem captives," the rabbi said. As I began to drift again, the rabbi lowered his voice. His intensity startled me awake. "Jews have inhabited Ethiopia since biblical times. Until recently, they kept steadfastly to the laws as they knew them, always dreaming of their return to Zion. But in the past few years, the Ethiopian government has forbidden Jewish practice and the teaching of Hebrew. They have arrested leaders as 'Zionist spies' and conscripted young boys into the army, never to return home."

Now I listened, spellbound. What did this have to do with redeeming captives?

The rabbi continued, "In recent years, like the Egyptians of Joseph's time, they faced famine-induced starvation. Thousands escaped to Sudan on foot, walking across the desert for months on end. At this very moment," he paused for emphasis, "an Israeli airlift is underway to bring them, 8,000 men, women and children, to their homeland."

My head whirled with the information that this was a cooperative effort among the Israel Defense Forces, the CIA, the U.S. embassy in Khartoum, mercenaries, and the Sudanese security forces. What an unlikely partnership!

"We have a unique opportunity," he concluded. "It takes six thousand dollars to redeem one Ethiopian Jew, six thousand dollars to save one Jewish life...."

Only six thousand dollars? To save a Jewish child? How many tens of thousands would I have given to save Ruth? During my twenty-five-minute walk home, all I could think about was the opportunity to save a Jewish life.

I burst through the door, and without saying hello launched into the story. "Julian, the rabbi told us about an operation to get Ethiopian Jews safely to Israel." Julian looked up from his book. "We have to do this," I told him. "We have an opportunity to save a Jewish life, and we have to do it." It didn't matter that the Ethiopian Jews were different from us in almost every dimension: cultural, educational, economic, and racial. As strangers in a strange land, they had clung to their faith in God and Torah for more than a millennium. They were Jewish. They were our people. And they needed our help. The amount, while far more than we had ever given to any single cause, seemed trifling compared to the opportunity *to save a Jewish child's life.*

The next night, Julian went to the public fund raising meeting. Though in those days he often ignored me or cut me off in mid-sentence, this time he listened. When it was his turn to speak out, he pledged "two thousand dollars for each member of my family"—ten thousand dollars. Despite his earlier assertion that he would act as if Ruth never had existed, this public declaration was probably a truer measure of his emotional state, a crack in the protective shell he had tried to create for himself.

I later learned that this generosity from a college professor inspired others in the room to do more than they had planned. Even Miriam, only fourteen at the time, donated $100 of her babysitting and birthday money. If there was one thing we Yudelsons had learned, it was the immeasurable value of a human life.

54

The issue of the value of our marriage was not nearly so easy to calculate. Shabbat, a day that had drawn us together, became a source of nails-on-the-blackboard friction. Twenty-plus years before, with Julian's encouragement, I had begun to light candles to welcome the "Sabbath Queen." We had often invited Shabbat guests and had always attended services together. Friday nights had evolved into family night. Julian read rabbinic tales aloud at dinner. We had time to discuss the weekly Torah portion, to play games with the children, to read, and still get to bed early. But now Larry and Miriam were less attentive to stories their father read. Julian and I found less and less to say to each other. Shabbat dinners became strained. I often went to services without Julian, who claimed they were void of intellectual or spiritual content. Our "Shabbat adventures" had fallen away when the children ceased riding in cars on Saturdays, and now I too refused to go canoeing or to a crafts fair if I had to drive to get there.

I was satisfied to walk to services with Miriam—the uninterrupted, undistracted mother-daughter time consoled me. Shabbat afternoons spent reading, napping, and walking with friends soothed me, but Julian complained about the "vibes" I emitted when he headed for the car. Not so, I insisted, and encouraged him to purchase a solo canoe. If he wouldn't observe Shabbat with me, at least he should have fun for himself. The first Saturday afternoon that he drove off, the canoe atop his car, Miriam and I stood at the window and cheered.

As Miriam and I grew closer, Julian seemed to grow more remote from us both. There is a Jewish story I first encountered in Martin Buber's *Tales of the Hasidim* that recounts that before Rabbi Zusya died, he said: "In the world to come they will not ask me, 'Why were you not Moses?' "They will ask me, 'Why were you not Zusya?'" I cringed each time I heard Julian say something to Miriam that suggested she wasn't being a good enough Ruth.

In addition to our Shabbat discord, we were plagued by Julian's unhappiness with work and life, my shedding the role of housewife to take a position in the workplace, and differences in the ways we continued to grieve. One day Julian moaned to me, "Your friends reach out to you. Nobody has helped me."

"Not true," I replied. "Why do you think David and Harvey started the study group with Jack? That was to support you in a way they thought you would find meaningful."

"But you've moved on and left me behind," he complained, not for the first time.

An image came to mind. "Look at it this way. We were both in the water, floundering. People threw two life rings. I clutched one and was barely able to hold on while a friend pulled me to shore. I didn't have the strength to reach for you; if I had tried, we'd have both drowned. And you didn't even move your hand toward the lifebuoy nearest you."

For the first time, Julian seemed to grasp that I, too, was barely surviving, that every day was a challenge, and that I didn't have the energy to salve his grief. With the help of an outstanding therapist, we hung on to our marriage by our toenails.

Once we were sure there would be a twenty-sixth anniversary, we planned a trip to England to celebrate our twenty-fifth.

That same summer, 1986, Miriam went on an NCSY tour of Israel.

The thought of Israel evoked my ever-ready tears. Ruth's greatest desire had been to visit Israel, and I had decided—though I hadn't let Julian in on my intentions—that we would take the girls to visit Larry during his planned post-high school study year. Ruth's death had intervened, and I couldn't face the idea of going without her. Perhaps I would, someday.

55

That winter, 1987, Larry, then twenty-two, joined his father and me in Atlanta for a family wedding. We stayed with my parents. A dozen years after the onset of Mom's illness, I missed the feisty lady who had chewed out my Sunday School teacher for suggesting that we light Sabbath candles. I missed the woman who insisted that she was a panentheist, not a pantheist, and carefully explained the distinction. (God pervades and animates the natural world vs. God is synonymous with nature.) Imagine my delight when her old self reappeared briefly during a heated discussion about kashrut.

On Friday night, Julian had driven to dinner with his siblings. Larry and I sat in the living room with my parents. "One of the most important decisions of David Ben Gurion, Israel's first prime minister, was that the Israeli army should keep the dietary laws," Larry said.

"That's terrible!" Mom blurted. "Those poor boys, deprived of bacon and ham."

I looked up, startled. I hadn't heard Mom speak so freely in years.

"Actually," Larry retorted, "it was wise. It meant that there wouldn't be distinctions between soldiers based on what foods they could eat."

"It was an awful decision," Mom objected.

Dad, uncomfortable with controversy, squirmed in his wingback chair.

After a long pause, I egged Larry on. "Did it work?"

"Actually, it did. The army is one of Israel's main unifying forces today. It's where recent immigrants can become truly Israeli, where religious and non-religious young people meet and live together. It was a wise decision."

"Those poor boys," Mom repeated.

Too soon, the discussion ran its course, but in those few minutes I had detected a glimmer of the mother I hadn't seen in more than a decade. How I wished I could suspend time and keep my "real mom" in the room!

Larry's statement seemed to have reached a place deep inside his grandmother to activate both a passionate response and her old love of an intellectual debate. What about kashrut triggered such a vehement, seemingly instinctive reaction? I wondered if, had she remained healthy, she would have come to see its value through my eyes. Would she have understood how kashrut binds a people together, even while separating them from others? Would she have grown to admire the discipline it instilled in her grandchildren?

How I yearned to return to my storybook life, when Mom was whole, when my sister lived, when Julian and I communicated comfortably, and when Ruth sparkled with possibility.

It may have been that trip or another that Dad assigned me the task of explaining to Mother a health-care directive. At one point, as we worked our way line by line through the document, she said, "So that means a doctor could kill me."

"No," I explained patiently to the mother who had majored in philosophy, read constantly, and been active in the League of Women Voters. "It means that if you have a disease like cancer, the doctors can't hook you up to machines to keep you alive." As I said this, I wondered how she felt about being alive at all. Did the birth of three additional grandsons since her brain surgery balance the death of her granddaughter? Did her husband's devotion compensate for the loss of independence? What could be worse than what she had lived through all these years? I never had the nerve to ask her, but found a hint in her comment some years before, "It should have been me" instead of Ruth.

While a neighbor witnessed my mother's left-handed signature on the health-care form, I felt torn by the process. It seemed to me that if a judge were to ask in a court of law if Mom understood what she signed, I'd have to say "no." But did it represent her wishes? I was convinced that it did.

Helping my mother with the health care directive reactivated that old series of questions that I usually kept carefully packed away: What divine purpose was served by the transformation of my mother from youthful vibrancy to hemiplegic, aphasic, wheelchair dependency? What purpose was served by Ruth's death? Was it, as so many rabbis told me, all God's will? If so, then what kind of a God …? Would I ever understand?

56

As I place newly purchased Hebrew-Russian Haggadot on the table along with our usual collection, I think about our guest list: Zigmund and Noyusha, Russian immigrants who landed in the United States barely two months ago; Russian friends who have been here long enough to translate; a dear friend who was a hidden child during the Holocaust, her husband, and a few other assorted friends and relatives.

With Galina translating, Julian gives an especially warm welcome to the newcomers. We proceed through the ceremony in a combination of Hebrew, English, Russian, and Yiddish.

"Avadim Hayinu," we sing. "We were Pharaoh's slaves in Egypt, and the Lord our God brought us forth from there with a mighty hand and an outstretched arm. And if the Holy One, blessed be he, had not brought our ancestors forth from Egypt, then we, our children, and our children's children would still be Pharaoh's slaves in Egypt."

Noyusha breaks into rapid Russian, which Galina translates. "This is my first seder since I was a very small child," she says in an emotional voice. "Without your help, we would still live in Russia. Slaves. Not free to be Jewish."

Throughout the evening, our discussions of freedom reverberate with a layered significance I suspect I will never forget. How can I ever again take for granted the opportunity to celebrate Passover?

* * *

For as long as I could remember, I had spoken of Judaism as "peoplehood," not just a religion. But that had been academic. Now I was beginning to feel connected in some almost mystical way with Jews I didn't know, Jews from the far-flung corners of the world, Jews like those from Ethiopia, and Jews like those in the Soviet Union. The Soviet Jews could neither practice their religion nor emigrate. If they applied to leave, they lost their jobs and risked being jailed as parasites. So when a rally to support Soviet Jewry was announced, Julian and I made plans to attend. At midnight on Saturday, December 5, 1987, we crowded onto a chartered bus headed to Washington, D.C. The gathering was timed for the day before Mikhail Gorbachev, president of the Soviet Union, would arrive for a two-day disarmament summit. The rally's organizers intended to place the emigration issue front and center on President Reagan's agenda for the meetings.

Sleepy excitement permeated the bus. Conversation died down as Rochester's lights faded behind us. Grateful for my short legs, I curled up, leaned against Julian, and slept off and on through the night. Sunlight roused me just as the bus pulled into a stadium parking lot near Washington. We joined the hordes walking toward the Metro station and then emerged from the underground train to see an ocean of faces.

"Do you think we know anyone in this mob?"

"We must." We jostled through the crowd until we spotted friends from Cleveland and Milwaukee.

"B.J.! Julian! How wonderful to see you!"

"We figured you'd be here. How have you..."

A roar drowned out our words. "Let my people go," 250,000 people shouted. We yelled with them, then turned back to our friends. A few minutes later, we again joined the chorus that screamed, "Let my people go."

"Let my people go," we called again and again. No matter that we could barely hear the speakers. No matter that the sun failed to warm the icy air or us. We were swept up in the energy of a quarter million voices demanding, as Moses had insisted to Pharaoh, "Let my people go." We were part of something vast and powerful. We were connected to everyone on that Mall and to all the Soviet Jews yearning for freedom.

We were one.

A few months after that historic demonstration, the leader of the Soviet Union opened the borders of his country for immigration to Israel. Several years later, two Russian immigrants celebrated their first seder in freedom with us. Fifteen years later, sitting in my sister's living room, a former Russian refusenik captivated me with a heavily accented account of his personal experiences. Some were tragic, all were arduous. He had finally managed to get out—after the Washington rally—and bring his then-fourteen-year-old daughter to this country. By the time he told me his story, his daughter was engaged to my nephew. We are one family.

57

It's the day before Passover, 1989. We are in Israel. Larry, who works here as a journalist, a stringer for the Long Island Jewish World, *has sent us to the market to buy produce for tonight's seder. Miriam, studying here for a year between high school graduation and college, holds out her hand. "Dad, give me twenty shekels, and both of you, stick close to me."*

From stall to stall she darts. We hurry after, keeping her faded denim skirt and print tee shirt in view, afraid of losing her in the throng of Passover shoppers. Strange aromas tickle my nose. Luscious colors and textures flash by in a rainbow-hued blur. My eyes widen as Miriam's small hands pick through the tomatoes until they hold the firmest and reddest. Quickly and confidently, she selects horseradish, cukes, strawberries, melon, and a plastic tablecloth. I listen in amazement as she bargains with the vendors in Hebrew. Half a year after I sent my little girl to the Holy Land to study Torah, she seems as comfortable on Jerusalem's streets as in the classroom.

We complete the shopping list and return to Larry's apartment. "Will you make the charoset?" he asks. Miriam and I set to work. When she was little, she often helped chop the apples and nuts. More recently, she made it by herself while I baked and cooked. It's fun to work together in Larry's tiny kitchen.

"You probably don't remember borrowing the Pomerantzes' nut chopper, do you?"

"Mom, I was only six when we moved from Cleveland to Rochester. But I've heard you talk about it."

"It was a relic from her grandmother's Pesach preparations. You and Ruth used to take turns moving the metal blades up and down in the glass container. Then when we moved, Phyllis gave me a similar one as a going-away present."

"And then you went modern with a food processor."

"I'm glad we don't have a food processor here. The only difference between this mortar and pestle you borrowed and ones in the Israel Museum is that this is brass and those are clay." I love this connection to my people across time as well as space.

Miriam finishes mashing the nuts. I add them to the hand-chopped apples, splash in some wine, and she sprinkles in a liberal dose of cinnamon. "Call Dad. We're ready for him to taste-test it."

Later, Miriam and I light candles. I look up and down the street through Larry's fourth floor window. At home, mine are the only holiday candles on the block. Here, in every apartment, pairs of flames flare into view. I suck in my breath and stare.

"Julian, come look!" He joins me at the open window, and we glow at our first sight of an entire neighborhood alight with the joyous celebration of our people's history.

Larry pushes us out to synagogue so that he can finish preparations alone. We follow a group of worshipers to a French congregation. The melodies are familiar, the cantor's Hebrew clear and easy to follow. This feels so comfortable, so different from thirty years ago, when I had totally embarrassed myself in the Lyon synagogue.

Two of Larry's friends join the four of us for the seder. Julian is in his element, guiding the discussion among a group of exceptionally intelligent, knowledgeable, and Jewishly committed young adults. The seder is long, even for us, but I'm free to listen, discuss and enjoy. I'm content to let my son be host, chief cook, and server.

When we get to the words Hashanah ha-ba-ah b'Yerushalaim, *next year in Jerusalem, we shout,* Hashanah ha-zot, *this year in Jerusalem!*

* * *

When I had written about Buber's view of Zionism almost thirty years before, I could never have imagined the emotional impact of celebrating Passover in the Promised Land. On the day after the seder, I prayed the morning service by myself on our hotel room balcony. The streets were empty save for groups walking to synagogue. A deep silence reigned: no slammed car doors, no traffic rumble, no honks. If I stood on my tiptoes in just the right spot and craned my neck, I could make out the Old City's walls in the distance. I once saw an antique map that showed Jerusalem as the center of the universe. That morning, in the stillness of the holiday, within walking distance of the Temple Mount, where two thousand years before people had offered their Passover sacrifices to God, I felt as if I were praying at the heart of the world.

At Larry's second seder that night, my candles looked lonely, no longer mirrored by twinkling flames throughout the neighborhood. Israelis keep only one day of festivals that are observed for two days in the Diaspora. (It has to do with how long it took, in ancient times, to carry the news of the sighting of the new moon, on the basis of which the festival days were determined.) The Bible instructs us to keep the "feast of unleavened bread" for seven days; on the first and last days "you shall have a holy convocation; you shall do no manner of servile work" (Lev. 23:7ff.). Today, outside of Israel, workaday activities are limited on the first two days, the seventh day and an additional eighth day. The country had resumed life; we were the outsiders, the visitors, who still had to play by Diaspora rules.

The next morning on the balcony, I found that the previous day's reverent silence had given way to typical weekday noise. I was unable to recapture the sacred feeling. But that first day had given me a taste of how it would feel to live in the majority, my Jewish rhythms in harmony with the world around me. This day, looking out over Jerusalem, I thought of Ruth's yearning to visit Israel. What would she say? How would she react? Would she be planning to live here one day? How would our lives all be different, if only…?

58

One night in our hotel room, Larry and Miriam began squabbling. I shuddered as they bickered like ten-year-olds about something inconsequential. Suddenly they looked at each other sheepishly and let their words drift off. It bothered me that even though they seemed to love sharing time together in Jerusalem, they could revert so easily into childhood patterns. On the other hand, perhaps it was a sign that they, at least, had returned to normalcy.

During the intermediate days of the weeklong Passover festival in Israel, the four of us traveled north with a private guide. Our itinerary was chosen, in part, to satisfy my craving to visit archaeological sites. At Beit Sean, we saw a well-preserved and restored Roman-Byzantine amphitheater. We visited Qasrin and its ancient synagogue. At Hazor, a site that dates to the Middle Bronze Age (1850-1650 BCE) and has later connections with Joshua and Solomon, we looked down toward the spring that had sustained people in biblical times. But looking wasn't enough for me. I felt compelled to follow the original stone steps all the way down to the source. I started down alone, but in my mind, I joined a line of young women… We step lightly down four flights of stairs that hug the sides of a square vertical shaft. We traverse a short tunnel to the spring, stoop down to fill our containers with water, then, jugs balanced on our heads or across our shoulders, trek back up the uneven staircase. Unlike the young women of my imagination, I pause to catch my breath and savor this bond with my past.

The next day we were in Tz'fat, home to mystics and artists. As the day waned, I returned to a synagogue we had visited that morning. Originally dating from the sixteenth century, it was rebuilt after an 1837 earthquake. We had admired its elaborate ark, carved from olive wood by an Eastern European craftsman, and its ornate chandeliers. Now I needed a place to say Kaddish for my sister, whose death a dozen years before had been on the fifth day of Pesach.

I was the only one in the family to observe her yahrzeit according to the Jewish calendar. Her children, our parents, and our younger sister consider April 7th, the day she died according to the secular calendar, to be the anniversary of her death. Now here I was in Israel, in a city considered holy by generations of Jews, prepared to remember her in the traditional way. Miriam and I located the entrance to the women's gallery around the corner on a side street, away from the main entrance. We tugged at the heavy door, but it was firmly locked. We retraced our steps. Speaking in Hebrew, Miriam asked the custodian to unlock the women's section.

"No." His Hebrew was too rapid for me to follow, but I caught the gist through his body language and Miriam's slower responses.

"My mother needs to say Kaddish for her sister's yahrzeit."

"No," he repeated. "*Lo tzarich.*" It's not necessary. Women don't say Kaddish.

I saw that we were collecting a gallery of onlookers. "It's okay," I told Miriam. "Don't make a scene. If I can't, I can't."

"Mom! Stay out of this! You want to, and he needs to let you." She turned back toward the man. "My mother is the only one who remembers her sister."

At this, he acquiesced. If no man said Kaddish, then perhaps.... Reluctantly, he led us around the corner, found the right key, and unlocked the door. I was as impressed with my daughter's spunk as I was disgusted with the custodian's old-fashioned views. When other women, probably tourists like ourselves, walked in and started praying, I felt vindicated that we had insisted. I loved this plucky side of Miriam.

We sat in the balcony overlooking the carved olive wood ark. As I prayed the familiar words, I felt myself surrounded by all the women who had ever prayed here. How many of them had said Kaddish for a beloved parent or cherished sister, in their hearts if not aloud? Had they prayed for the health of a sick child? For the matchmaker to find the perfect husband?

I stood to praise God in the words of the Kaddish: "*Yitgadal v'yitkadash...*" I was no longer a tourist hearing the synagogue's history and admiring its beauty. Praying here put me inside the story. Now I, too, had a personal history in Tz'fat.

Two days later, back in Jerusalem, we attended services at the Great

Synagogue. I was pleased that I could follow the service, except for the Hebrew sermon, but found it too formal and ostentatious for my taste. The next morning, because the festival had ended the previous day for Israelis, I once again prayed by myself on our hotel balcony. The sights and sounds of Jerusalem mingled with the psalms of praise I recited. The warm Israeli sun seemed to penetrate my very soul.

On our first trip to Israel, seventeen years earlier, leaving our three young children with my parents, we had come as tourists. I had been struck by the beauty, variety, and vibrancy of the tiny country, but it had been as a visitor to an exotic locale. We had returned this time to spend Passover with our son and daughter, each living for a year in this place. This trip deepened our sense of connection with the land and its people. Now I felt myself to be truly a part of its history, a link in the generations that had lived and prayed in this holy land.

59

For fifteen years, Dad had cared for Mom at home. He had installed a chairlift and made other physical accommodations to their two-story home. Thankfully, he had been able to employ a nurse eight hours a day, and in recent years, had added a sleep-in housekeeper to help with nighttime chores. But on a visit soon after our return from Israel, I saw disturbing changes: Mother's overall condition seemed worse. She called out for Dad throughout the night, and he, now in his early eighties, was exhausted. Because it felt as if I might lose him as well as her, I was not unhappy when he proposed moving her to a nursing home. Rather, I encouraged his decision. I suspect that for Mom, though, this was a sign, perhaps even a welcome one, that she could let go. She soon stopped eating and was transferred to the hospital.

Fortunately, I arrived in Atlanta for a Yudelson-side bat mitzvah that same day. As I perched on the bed beside her, she said to me repeatedly, "I am going to die." I sought to reassure her, missing the point at first that she meant, "I want to die. I plan to die. I am going to make sure that I die." Before my scheduled return flight on Monday, I sat beside Dad in the doctor's office. The physician had verified Mother's cogency, and in accordance with her wishes, backed by the health care directive I had walked her through, agreed to remove the feeding tube that had been inserted when she first refused to eat. His instructions: encourage feeding, but don't force it. Dad and I squeezed hands. I knew he was both heartbroken and relieved.

A week later, after fifteen years of a dependence she hated, my once-spirited mother managed a final spunky act: she starved herself to death.

I was sad, but my reaction to Ruth's death had become my yardstick for grief, and on that scale, my sorrow was barely measurable. Because I had never stopped longing for the mother with whom I felt a powerful, emotional bond, my pain for the replacement mother was easier to handle.

Mom died late Saturday night, June 30, 1990. I arrived in Atlanta Sunday afternoon. Dad greeted me with the information that we had an appointment at the funeral home in a few minutes. Before I had put my suitcase down, he asked, "What dress should I take to bury her in?"

"Nothing wrong with a white shroud," I replied.

Dad shuddered, and I did not persist. I would have been comfortable following the ancient tradition of burial in a plain shroud within a simple pine coffin, a reminder that we are all equal in death. But Dad was in charge; my role was not to insist on a tradition that he didn't accept but to honor my parents by supporting him.

After he and my sister (who had arrived the day before) had chosen a favorite dress, the three of us went to the funeral home. Margaret and I encouraged the plainest coffin there; Dad opted for something a bit more substantial.

By the time we returned home, friends filled the house. Although I knew that this would not be the traditional mourning period to which I had become accustomed—seven days of staying home, receiving guests, and focusing on the deceased as the first step toward healing—I was taken aback by the lack of consideration for our feelings. Yes, Mom had been ill a long time. But that didn't mean I was ready to socialize. Several family friends invited me to enjoy their swimming pool or to come to their Fourth of July picnic. My mother wasn't even buried yet, and they were inviting me to a social occasion. Although they meant well, they offended my now-traditional sensibilities.

My parents' rabbi, who had been Mom's student during her one disastrous (or so she had told me) year of teaching Sunday school, was vacationing in Alaska. His young assistant at Atlanta's oldest Reform temple detected that I was more observant than the family. She responded by including some of the more traditional rituals, which were unfamiliar to the few close friends and relatives who came with us to the cemetery.

The grassy hills were scorched yellow-brown, the air sluggish. The pallbearers, Dad's cronies, lined up like a cartoon of shriveled crows under the searing sun. At the conclusion of the service, the rabbi tried to get the guests into two lines. The point is for the family to walk between the rows, surrounded, as they leave the cemetery, by words of solace, "May the Omnipresent comfort you among the mourners of Zion and Jerusalem." But these folks didn't know the choreography. They formed a single line. The rabbi asked half to move opposite them, and they all switched sides. I don't think they ever made two columns. Through my tears, I smiled at both their loving intentions and their humorous missteps.

Over and over I was struck by how far I had traveled from my Reform roots. Traditional Judaism gives the family time to mourn, surrounded by those who come to offer consolation. I had learned to enter a house of mourning with my ears and eyes open, my heart full, and my mouth shut. I had learned that mourners don't want to chit-chat, that a simple "I'm sorry" or a hug can be eloquent, and that a personal memory of the deceased is a gift to the bereaved.

One day during shiva, two women who looked vaguely familiar conversed on the sofa. With my sister Margaret, I moved the low ottoman on which I sat close to them. "How did you know our mother?" we asked.

"She was in our League of Women Voters unit," said one.

"We played golf together," answered the other.

They turned to each other and resumed the dialogue we had interrupted.

We had hoped these old friends could help return us to a time when

Mom's closet had been filled with golf shirts, party dresses, and designer shoes, rather than the twenty-three bed jackets we found. Instead, their response demonstrated to me the difference between a condolence call and a traditional shiva visit. They were doing the "nice" thing, stopping by to offer sympathy. We needed the mitzvah of consolation, which in this case meant to help us remember our mother as she had been in the long-gone days when she had been their active and vivacious friend.

Margaret and I decided to return to our respective homes for the final days of shiva. If my Rochester visitors had ever met my mother, it was only as an old lady in a wheelchair. They couldn't share any memories of better, more active times, but they could—and did—give me the opportunity to talk, to cry, and to tell them about the mother who had raised me. Once again, I thanked God for my caring community.

60

In 1991, as Julian and I approached our 30th wedding anniversary, our children decided to correct a glaring omission. One of the key elements of a Jewish marriage had long been missing: I lacked the protection of a ketubah, a marriage contract, which spelled out my husband's moral, legal, and financial obligations to me.

Yes, we had been wed in a Jewish ceremony, and no one questioned the validity of our marriage, but there had been no ketubah. The certificate that Rabbi Rothschild had casually handed us in 1961 bore no similarity to the contract that would have been signed, witnessed, and read at a traditional ceremony. Although today a man may joke about how many goats and sheep his wife is worth (the listing of these particulars is integral to the proper text of a traditional marriage contract), historically the ketubah had marked a great leap forward in protecting a woman's rights.

On a Sunday morning in June 1991, we gathered with our closest friends. Miriam had engaged a young cousin to create the document with Hebrew calligraphy and artwork that incorporated our children's names as well as loons—those beautiful black and white waterfowl for which Julian and I search on northern lakes—and the walled city of Jerusalem. Rabbi Kilimnick, sensitive to the fact that we already were an old married couple, and not young, nervous newlyweds, used the text for a couple that has lost their ketubah. He led Julian through an affirmation that he had married me on June 25, 1961, but that we no longer had a ketubah. Next he instructed our two chosen witnesses to sign their Hebrew names, attesting to Julian's statement. Then he read the text, giving our long marriage the Jewish seal of approval.

"It's about time!" joked a friend.

Another turned to Larry and Miriam. "I guess you're legitimate now!"

For me it was both a sign that I expected this marriage to last, despite our shaky years, and a symbol of my ongoing ascent up the ladder of tradition.

61

Another year, another seder. Larry has brought his girlfriend from New York City, but Miriam is with her fiance's family across town. I wish they were with us, too.

It's time for the four questions. No young children this year. Larry, Susan, and an RIT graduate student establish that Larry is the youngest. The last time I remember his asking the questions was before Ruth was old enough. He couldn't have been more than six or seven. Back then, he sang the traditional words and tune in a high voice. But tonight he reads the questions in the mature voice of a 27-year-old man.

"Mah-nishtanah. Nishtanah. Hmmmm, that's the reflexive form of L'shanot, to change. What is it about this night that causes me to change myself? How is this night transformative in a way that other nights aren't?"

For fifty years, I've read or heard the four questions, sometimes in English, sometimes in Hebrew. I've never heard them like this. Larry's thoughtful analysis of the Hebrew grammar suggests serious self-examination rather than a springboard for discussion—although his question alone sparks a thirty-minute discussion.

I've often thought about how different our seders are from the ones I grew up with. For the first time I consider how our seders have changed me.

While I ponder, Julian points to the lamb shank, the matzah, and the bitter herbs, each with its explanation. Now it's my turn to read. "In every generation one must look upon himself as if he personally had come out from Egypt…" Well, I think, this is certainly one way the seders have helped transform me. I guess this line was in the Haggadah we used when I was young, but it didn't mean anything to me. Now I feel connected to those ancient Israelites. I truly believe that I came out of Egypt and stood at Mt. Sinai along with all generations of Jews, past and future.

* * *

I used to turn all my worries over to my mother-in-law, figuring that since she, the stereotypical Jewish mother, was going to worry anyway, she might as well include my concerns. Since Ruth's death, I had adopted one sister-in-law's mantra that whatever you don't worry about is what happens. I tried to cover all bases by fretting about everything—the way I had heard Miriam's husband talk to her; their late-night long-distance drives; Miriam's pregnancy; Larry's life in New York City, with its high crime rate, and on and on.

Despite these anxieties, a decade after Ruth's death I was functioning again. My depressed days were, thank God, behind me. I went to work, smiled, laughed, and probably seemed normal to everyone but myself. But the underlying pain colored my outlook; it was never far from the surface. Ruth used to laugh at me because I could watch only the last three minutes of "Little House on the Prairie" and tear up at the sappy ending. I had always cried easily, but I no longer pretended that moist eyes derived from allergies. If I hadn't earned the right to weep, who had?

And of course, Ruth's death had scarred me more deeply that any anti-Semitic incident from my youth ever had. I felt myself an outsider in a world of happy, intact families.

But cautious and fearful as I had become, I couldn't resist the excitement brought on by Miriam's phone call on the afternoon before Shmini

Atzeret, the 8th day of Sukkot, in 1994. She was in the hospital, in labor three weeks before her due date. The impending holiday posed a communications problem because neither she nor her husband would use the telephone after sunset.

"I've arranged for a nurse to call if it's after Shmini Atzeret begins. You'll hear the message over the answering machine. Don't worry, I'll talk to you later."

Don't worry? How could I not? I slept that night with one ear open, waiting for the phone call that never came.

In the morning, I left home reluctantly, but once underway, I almost ran the mile and a half to shul. My first grandchild was about to be born, and I was eager to sing God's praises. At one point, I found myself skipping exuberantly. A joyous shriek burst from my mouth. Was it okay to be this excited when the baby wasn't even born yet?

At other times, a knot of fear reminded me that my family and I were not exempt from things that go awry. "Man plans, God laughs," I reminded myself. I wondered if a woman in labor should be included in the special prayer for the sick.

I arrived, breathless, at the start of Hallel. "Blessed are You, Lord our God… who has commanded us to recite the Hallel." Praise poured from my heart.

"He makes the woman in a childless house a happy mother of children. Hallelujah!" These words at the end of Psalm 113 leapt off the page. I didn't remember ever noticing them before. Oh Miriam, I thought, may your child bring you as much happiness as you bring me.

I focused on the words. "Why, mountains, did you skip like rams, and you, hills, like lambs? It was at the presence of the Lord, Creator of the earth…." The familiar verse came alive. Like the hills and mountains, I could barely contain myself.

Miriam, "May the Lord give you increase: you and your children. May you be blessed by the Lord" with a healthy child. My overall excitement pushed the niggling fear to the back of my mind.

"Hodu l'Adonai, ki tov, ki l'olam hasdo. Sing praises to God, for He is good, for his mercy endures forever." These words were so much easier for me now than they had been in my time of rending questions. And

then to a melody that always moves me, "This is the day the Lord has made. Let us rejoice and be glad in it."

How many times had I cried my way through those words? How many times had I struggled to praise God in the thirteen years since Ruth's death? But on September 27, 1994, I recited them with the psalmist's fervor. I felt as if I were in a Chagall painting, soaring over the pews, buoyed by anticipation, wonder, and gratitude.

Julian, who had stayed home to await the call, joined our hosts and me on our way to their home for lunch after services. "No news," he reported. "The phone never rang."

My sense that the baby was emerging as the psalms sprang from my lips was, apparently, just a fantasy. I fidgeted through lunch, eager to get home and check the answering machine.

A blinking red dot greeted us. Julian started to reach for it, knowing that I did not use electricity on Shabbat or holidays. But maternal instinct won out over commandments, and with a deliberate motion, I punched "play." A stranger's voice told us that Miriam's daughter had arrived at 10:30 that morning, about the time that I was reciting Hallel.

The next day, Simhat Torah, was a day to rejoice—in the Torah and in our granddaughter. We had to wait until the two-day holiday ended to talk to the new parents. How was Miriam? How big was the baby? Did she have hair? What color?

Three days later, Julian and I drove to Baltimore to meet our first grandchild, who had, I felt, been borne into life on the wings of my prayers. As I counted Leah's fingers, absorbed her delicious scent, and gently kissed the reddish wisps on her head, I marveled at the miracle I held in my arms. How could such a tiny being, whose five pounds I could barely feel, fill my heart so completely?

"This is the Lord's doing. It is wondrous in our eyes. Hallelujah!"

62

When Leah was eight months old, I drove to Baltimore for Mother's Day weekend. Julian was stuck at home grading final exams, but Larry, still single, planned to join Miriam and me. He was eager to view an exhibit that was closing soon at the Jewish Museum of Maryland, where Miriam was educational director. The exhibit was about the Jews of Ichenhausen, Germany, the birthplace of my mother's maternal grandmother. A portrait of *her* grandmother, my great-great-great-grandmother, Fannie Koschland, hung in my parents' home.

Six hours after I left Rochester, I met Miriam at the museum and gave her a bear hug. I still couldn't quite believe that my baby was a mother. We didn't have as much contact as I would have liked. My visits to see Leah had been less frequent than I preferred, because Miriam's husband, Alan, seemed to want to control her contact with her family and appeared to resent my visits. When Miriam had told me he was working nights, I felt more comfortable coming for this weekend visit.

Larry called from the train station. As we drove to pick him up, I commented to Miriam that she seemed to have lost the last of her baby fat.

"I haven't done it the best way," she confided. "I've been depressed. Alan's abusive, and I'm thinking of leaving the marriage." Her words tumbled out and landed like an avalanche on my heart.

Although I had never considered this relationship, which began as a teenage romance, to be a good partnership, I hadn't expected this. But the small issues of discomfort that I had brushed away in my desire to see my daughter happy began to fit together now. I hadn't liked the way I had heard Alan speak to her. And now that I considered, he had driven a wedge between her and our family. I had kept quiet, knowing that married couples have to work out their own relationships. There had been one puzzling late-night phone call when she had whispered, "I need a hug." "You've got it," I had replied hastily before I heard the click that meant she had hung up. Should I have called back? Should I have probed what that meant? Not knowing, I had responded to her frightened voice with silence.

Now, as the picture came into focus, I mumbled something about being profoundly sorry about the situation and tremendously proud of her for facing up to the truth.

"Don't say anything to Larry," Miriam requested as she maneuvered through Baltimore's traffic. Though a flock of questions pecked at me, I waited for Miriam to talk. We had barely begun our conversation when we were at the station greeting Larry.

Back at the museum, Miriam and I ignored the looming present while we three immersed ourselves in our roots.

"When I've given tours of the museum," Miriam explained, "I've pointed out this self-guided show, but I haven't been through it myself. I don't understand why you care so much about it, Larry. I don't see what it has to do with us."

I picked up the sole English translation of the panels prepared in German by current residents of Ichenhausen and began reading aloud. The third or fourth panel illustrated the town's Jewish section. Houses were labeled with their owners' names. I pointed to two houses on the primitively drawn chart. "Koschland. That's us! Granny's mother was a Koschland." If I stared long enough, could I will my ancestors to come to the door?

We continued to the next wall. A panel gave statistics. "Look, here we are again. In 1845, there were more than 1,000 Jewish residents. In 1853, there were only 718."

"That's when we came over." Larry shared my excitement.

"Mmmm," my daughter replied, distracted from the Koschlands' long-ago flight to new opportunities by the one she was contemplating.

A half hour later, the three of us stood in front of the last panel, a list of town residents deported in the 1940s. Together we scanned the list. Koschland, Jakob. Koschland, Heinz. Koschland.... I hadn't known that I had lost relatives in the Holocaust. These cousins were distant, to be sure, but they were mine...and my children's.

Eyes wet, I looked at my daughter. I thought I was crying for my lost ancestors. Did I also weep for Miriam's loss? For the pain she endured? For the hard times to come?

"OK, Mom, I get it. It does have something to do with me," she said about the exhibit. But there were a lot of things that I didn't get.

63

Back at Miriam's apartment, I picked up my adorable granddaughter, who snuggled into my arms. She was beautiful and alert, with a ready smile. After a few minutes, I reluctantly released her to her doting uncle so that I could help Miriam prepare for Shabbat. Whenever Larry left the room, Miriam and I exchanged furtive whispers. There was so much I wanted to ask, to know, but I had to let her tell me her own way, in her own time. And I knew I had to respect her request for privacy.

Larry looked on while Miriam and I lit our Shabbat candles. Silently, I prayed not only for her physical safety but for her mental strength. I ached for the baby nestled in her arms.

Miriam, her husband Alan, Larry, and I began the Sabbath meal by singing *Shalom Aleichem:* Welcome, angels of the Most High, enter in peace, bless me with peace, go in peace. Peace. *Shalom bayit,* household peace. The irony was overwhelming.

Alan sang the Hebrew verses from Proverbs traditionally recited to a woman on Friday nights: "A woman of valor, who can find?... Her husband's heart trusts in her . . . She brings him good, not harm, all the days of her life. . . . her husband praises her... Many women have excelled, but you surpass them all."

Didn't Alan realize what he sang every week? He sang it in Hebrew, a language he didn't understand, but surely he understood the sense of the verses. How could he sing this to Miriam with a straight face when at other times he insulted her, punched her, or—I later learned—threw the remote control at her, missing his baby's head by inches and giving his wife a black eye? What was the sense in the ritual if it didn't connect to his actions?

Kiddush followed. Holding the wine cup aloft, Alan chanted the traditional words of praise to God for creating the world and for bringing us out of Egypt. "Blessed are you, Lord…who has made us holy through your commandments."

How could a man who abused his wife talk about holiness? The question my father used to ask when we talked about my increasing religious observance nagged at me: What difference do the rituals make as long as you're a good person? "Why should it be either-or?" I had responded. Now I also saw the question in reverse—what good do the rituals do if you're *not* a good person?

On Sunday's drive home to Rochester, I had an unwelcome passenger: worry. This wasn't niggling, back-of-the-mind, worry-so-bad-stuff-doesn't-happen concern. This was anxiety. Some Mother's Day gift! I explained the situation to Julian, reminding him that acting on his violent impulse to protect his daughter would likely land him in jail and only burden Miriam further. Instead, we needed to support her in any way she asked.

Two months later, in July 1995, Julian and I met Larry, Miriam, and baby Leah in Atlanta, on our way to a Heyman family reunion at a resort ninety miles south. By then, Miriam had moved into her own apartment. Alan was not with us.

The cousins, whose planning for this sixty-person event had begun with a save-the-date card two years earlier, responded to my food concerns. "Everyone will bring their own food to share for Friday night and Shabbat lunch," they had told me. "We'll have kosher food for your family at Saturday night's official reunion banquet." Our first stop was at a kosher butcher and deli, where we stocked up before driving our rented van to Callaway Gardens.

The entire weekend was a magnificent confirmation of the values of family closeness and communal responsibility taught by my grandparents and passed on by my father and his three siblings. Dad, the youngest and only still-living member of his generation, reveled in the role of patriarch.

Throughout, I noticed how relaxed Miriam looked, how comfortably she interacted with her brother and cousins. "You know," she told me the last day, "if Alan had been here, I'd have spent the whole time defending him to my family and explaining my family to him. This weekend confirms that I've made the right decision."

For me the most memorable experience was not our Saturday night banquet (with pre-packaged airline-style meals for those of us who had requested kosher food). It was not the entertaining array of songs and doggerel with which, according to longstanding family tradition, we described our lives to each other. It was not even the pleasure of being with my cousins, watching our children renew old relationships and seeing how well the youngest ones played together. Rather, it was our joint Friday night dinner. We set out an assortment of food on picnic tables near the swimming pool. Then we women lit our Shabbat candles. Not just Miriam and I, but three-quarters of the women welcomed the Sabbath together. And this was no just-for-show candle lighting. We all sang the blessings with the comfort of weekly familiarity.

Julian had been asked to recite kiddush for the group. He stood, raised the wine cup, and began in Hebrew, "*Va-y'hi erev va-y'hi boker yom ha shishi,*" "And it was evening and it was morning the sixth day…." At the point at which people often join in, my family, my extended family, my extended *Reform* family, lifted their voices. *You have chosen us and hallowed us above all nations, and have graciously given us the holy Sabbath as a heritage. Blessed are You, O Lord who sanctifies the Sabbath.*

I glanced around at my cousins, their children, and their grandchildren. Most had been raised in Reform homes similar to mine. A few, who had married into the family, came from more traditional backgrounds. A couple of the younger ones were not Jewish. But virtually all knew kiddush. They sang it with gusto. I realized that though I may have journeyed further than most in my family, Reform Judaism itself had not stood still. Rituals that had been considered antiquated when I was a child had reassumed their place within Reform practice, connecting these Reform Jews with their past and with other Jews around the globe.

As my heart swelled at this realization, my eyes moved to my 86-year-old father. He sat silently on a picnic bench, his mouth agape, his eyes confused. I could almost see his thoughts, "How do all my nieces and nephews, great-nieces and great-nephews, members of Reform temples, know these prayers? I thought it was just B.J. and her family who did this. You mean she's not the only crazy one? What has happened to *my* Reform Judaism?"

And yet, given a choice of my father's ethics or my son-in-law's seemingly empty ritual observances, I'd still go with Dad. He may never have recited kiddush or serenaded my mother with "A Woman of Valor," but for 55 years their home was blessed with love and respect, even after Mom's stroke robbed them of true companionship.

64

A few months later, I drove to Baltimore to be with Miriam when she received her *get,* the final step in a Jewish divorce. While Judaism traditionally sees marriage as made in heaven, it recognizes that not all marriages work on earth. We arrived at the rabbi's home at the appointed hour. Two rabbis plus a scribe trained in the intricacies of preparing the divorce document set a somber mood in their black coats, long beards and black skullcaps. I was grateful that I could be there to support Miriam in this all-male environment.

"Where's Alan?" I whispered to Miriam. The *get* must be given by the man; the ritual could not proceed without him. "What if he doesn't show up?"

"He wouldn't be the first man who refused to give a *get.* It's all about control, you know." Her voice betrayed her nervousness.

At last a knock on the door broke the tension. Alan entered. Even he, usually talkative and seeking center stage, was subdued by the laden atmosphere.

Because each *get* must be handwritten in Aramaic for the specific man and woman involved, the scribe first checked and double-checked the Hebrew names, then meticulously composed the document according to the ancient formula. It stated Alan's intent to "release, discharge, and divorce" Miriam.

Following the rabbi's instructions, Alan took the paper, held it up, and repeated the words, "This is your divorce. Accept this document of divorce and with this you are divorced from me from here on. You are now permitted to marry any man." He dropped the document into Miriam's outstretched hands. Miriam closed her fingers around it and lifted it up. She then put it under her arm and walked the ritual few feet, symbolically accepting the document.

The ceremony was complete. According to Jewish law, Miriam was now free to marry another man. More importantly, she was liberated from Alan.

"Thank you," Miriam mumbled and turned toward the door.

"Thank you," I said to the rabbis and scribe.

I opened the door, and Miriam's mouth twitched into a smile. We stepped onto the front stoop, and a grin brightened her face. As we started down the front steps, Miriam reached for the hat she had worn as a married woman and tossed it high into the air.

65

One Shabbat in 1995, I sat in services with a friend's daughter who was in Rochester to visit her parents. It was the Orthodox shul where Ruth had led the children's service years before, a synagogue I attended only rarely because the memories were too painful. Of the numerous sermons I have heard over the years, I remember few. Of those, I recall some for their inspiration, others for their instruction. Sometimes I've agreed, sometimes I've disagreed. But this one left me outraged.

That day happened to be the bar mitzvah service of a boy who had emigrated with his parents from Russia. I think the rabbi was trying to convey the importance of being, practicing, and staying Jewish. As he began to discuss the evils of intermarriage (to a boy of thirteen, no less!), I turned toward my young friend.

Her siblings had both married Jews, yet were not especially observant. She, married to a non-Jew, attended synagogue regularly and visited a nursing home on Saturday afternoons to study the Torah portion with a woman immobilized by MS.

"And which of the three of you is most observant?" I murmured.

She gave a tight, ironic smile.

The rabbi continued, "A bad Jewish marriage is better than a good intermarriage."

My friend stood, muttered an apology to me, and walked out. I stayed, but have rarely set foot in that synagogue since, even though several rabbis have come and gone since that day.

Did the rabbi really not understand the depths to which a bad marriage can sink? Had he never encountered, had he not read of, Jewish marriages in which unacceptable slaps or pinches escalate into beatings that produce black eyes and bruised souls, in which one spouse makes the other feel worthless, diminished, no longer "in the image of God"? If he didn't know of such a Jewish marriage, I certainly did.

Thank God, I thought, my precious Leah will not grow up in a destructive household with no love, no peace, no respect. Yes, she will spend part of her time with her dad—and I pray she will be safe—but Miriam, who has integrated her grandparents' ethical and respectful world view with her own commitment to tradition, will be her primary influence.

Perhaps this rabbi didn't understand the human cost of a bad Jewish marriage, a cost so high that neither pious prayers nor stringent ritual observances could compensate. Wasn't the point of daily prayers to remind us of our obligations to pursue justice, to walk humbly with God and God's creation? The question haunted me, even as I continued to find value, comfort, and meaning in my community.

66

In December 1995, Miriam deposited fifteen-month-old Leah with us on her way to a friend's wedding in Buffalo. Months earlier, before their divorce, Miriam and her husband had both agreed to be in the bridal party. "I dread being near him all weekend," she groaned. I understood her distress, but was thrilled that she had entrusted Julian and me with our precious granddaughter.

A few days later, she was back in my kitchen, this time smiling broadly. "I've met a man I can talk to more comfortably than anyone I've ever known."

"Whoaaaa," I admonished her. "You haven't had time to figure out who you are, and what's more, your civil divorce isn't even final."

"Don't worry, Mom. He lives in California. I'll probably never see him again."

Nine months later, my headstrong daughter drove with her toddler from their Baltimore apartment to our Rochester home for Rosh Hashanah. Michael, her California beau, flew in for the holiday. I was touched that Miriam was bringing him to meet us, naively thinking that she wanted our approval, until I learned that it was Leah whose acceptance she sought. Leah seemed to sense that this stranger was going to be someone special in her life, and at barely two years old ran into his arms with a huge grin.

Michael, an Orthodox rabbi, was the Hillel Foundation program director on a Los Angeles area college campus. Though, like Miriam, he had not been raised in an Orthodox home—his father was a Conservative rabbi—he shared her deep commitment to traditional practice combined with an open outlook on the world. He seemed solid, reliable, and determined to take loving care of our daughter.

In the summer of 1997, Julian and I went to Israel with Miriam and Leah to meet Michael's parents, who had moved there years before. When we weren't with his family, we explored Jerusalem with a leisure we had never experienced in this golden place. Michael led us through the narrow, cobblestone streets of the old city with an assurance born of having lived in Israel from ages seven to fourteen and then again during his college years at Israel's Bar Ilan University. We happened on a street carnival with balloons and clowns that excited Leah, now two and a half. I took in the aromas of middle eastern spices wafting from windows, the Hebrew sounds all around me, and the sunlight reflecting off stone buildings.

At the top of the stairs leading down to the Kotel, the Western Wall, I paused to look out at the city I was growing to love. Off to the right I could make out the Mount of Olives, where Jews have been buried from biblical times until today. In the distance, church steeples poked up above surrounding buildings, and opposite me, commanding the skyline, was the golden Dome of the Rock. Julian and I had been inside this mosque on our first trip to Israel in 1972. Now, twenty-five years later, Jews were not allowed in its vicinity.

Julian carried the stroller and Michael carried Leah down the long flight of steps, through an airport-like security check, to the plaza filled with Israelis and tourists. Miriam, Leah, and I approached the section of the Wall reserved for women and worked our way toward the front. Involuntarily, my hand caressed the stones that date from King Herod's rebuilding of the Temple's foundations. Despite the fiery June sun, they were cool and hard beneath my fingers. Wherever a bit of dirt had found its way into the cracks, small gray-green, dry-looking bushes grew as if out of the stones themselves. Doves cooed overhead, occasionally landing on greenery high up the wall. This is a metaphor for my people's history, my history, I thought, this life growing out of the stones, existing beyond all odds, taking advantage of every drop of moisture to take root where no life should exist.

And these were my people, these women jostling their way through the crowd to the wall itself: these old ladies in "babushkas" and dark, printed housedresses, these teenagers wearing the yeshiva girls' uniform of a long denim skirt with a long-sleeved white blouse buttoned to the collar, these tourists in fashionable jeans with oversized handbags, snapping pictures. Ordinary Israeli women, dressed for work or home, breathed their afternoon prayers directly into the stones. Their whispered entreaties seemed to mingle with the bits of paper spilling out of every crack in the wall. The folded or rolled scraps carried petitions to God, prayers that expressed the collective yearning of the Jewish people.

Ruth's dearest dream had been to visit Israel. The recollection of her unfulfilled longing saddened me. If only she had lived long enough. If only…

Leah tugged at my hand, and my heart lightened. Church bells tolled, the muezzin called, cars honked beyond the Dung Gate, strains of Hebrew song rang out in youthful voices. I ran my fingers over the ancient stones one last time, and with my granddaughter at my side, I backed respectfully away from the wall.

Six months later, on the January 1998 morning of Miriam and Michael's wedding day, Miriam, Leah, and I again stood at the Kotel. In one hand, Miriam held the small prayer book she had received as a bat mitzvah gift. In the other rested Leah's tiny fingers. It was a moving image, the ancient stones a backdrop to mother and child. I suspect Miriam's prayers were for their future happiness with the man she would marry that evening.

I thanked God that she had found someone with whom she seemed to share so much, whose family we liked, and who radiated love for Miriam's young daughter.

Two days later, Julian and I sat in our hotel room with the bride and groom, Leah, Larry, and Larry's girlfriend, Eve. We chatted about the day's activities. After a few minutes, Larry spoke up. "Nobody's asked us what we did today," he said.

"Okay, Larry, I'll bite," I responded quickly. "What did you do today?"

"We got engaged!"

"You did *what?*" I jumped up to hug Eve and Larry.

"Mazel tov!"

"Tell us about it!"

Larry's response to our volley of questions floated through the room. "I took Eve to the most beautiful site in Jerusalem, the *tayelet,* the promenade that overlooks the city."

"He handed me a book of Yehuda Amichai love poetry. He had inscribed it with his proposal." Eve's voice expressed the wonderment we all felt.

My son, the romantic! What more perfect place to propose a life together than the spot from which, according to Jewish legend, God showed Abraham where one day his descendants would build their holy city.

In our week in Jerusalem, our family had expanded to include a new son, a soon-to-be daughter, and three additional grandchildren from Eve's first marriage. Being in Israel deepened our sense of blessing and holiness.

67

Dad's 90th birthday celebration brought the entire family together again in the fall of 1998. Miriam and Michael arrived in Atlanta early on the red eye from Los Angeles. I worried about Dad's first meeting with his new grandson-in-law. Although Michael did not lead a congregation, he *was* an Orthodox rabbi. Dad had long since forgiven Larry for his youthful mishandling of Shabbat, but I knew that he had not forgotten.

I counted on Dad to be a gentleman and respectful; he always was. But I also knew that he could ask tough, direct questions. He was bound to ask about his perceived conflict between the prophetic ideals with which he had been raised—caring for the less fortunate, pursuing justice, treating people with respect and integrity—and the ritual traditions based in the five books of Moses and interpreted by the rabbis. "Why," he asked me again and again, "does it matter if you turn on electricity on the Sabbath as long as you're a good person?" Would Michael's answer measure up?

I wish I had been there to witness the scene Miriam later described to me. It must have gone something like this:

Dad sat in his favorite wingback chair. Miriam and Michael perched, less at ease, on the couch.

"Well, Michael, I understand you're an Orthodox rabbi."

"That's true."

"Tell me then, which do you think is more important, the fourth commandment or the fifth?"

Michael looked sidelong at Miriam, who had warned him about Granddad's concern. He hesitated just a second, then spoke in a low, respectful voice. "I once knew a rabbi who helped many teenagers become more observant. He used to tell them, 'If keeping Shabbos starts a fight with your parents, then you're not doing it right.'"

"So honoring your parents is more important?"

"Noooo, I'm not saying that. What I mean is that there are ways to handle virtually any situation that respects both. I run into this with some of my students, and I see my job as helping the ones who want to become more observant to do it without damaging family relationships."

Miriam squeezed Michael's hand. Granddad considered Michael's words. He nodded, then moved on to friendlier subjects.

When Miriam told me this story, I asked if she thought Michael's answer had satisfied her grandfather.

"Sort of," she said. "I think he got it that the two commandments shouldn't conflict. But I'd say it was a grudging acceptance."

That weekend, a few of us observed Shabbat in the midst of the family hubbub while all of us, three generations of Dad's descendants, paid homage to our patriarch.

68

The next spring, Dad planned to attend two back-to-back Elderhostel programs in southern California with his steady companion, Martha. In between, they would celebrate the Israelites' exodus from Egypt at a seder at Miriam and Michael's home. I warned Dad to eat a hearty late-afternoon snack because lengthy discussion would precede the festive meal.

"What is there to discuss at a seder?" Dad asked. I smiled inwardly at his naiveté. A parade of seders past flashed through my mind. I could hear Larry sing-songing the four questions that he had memorized in kindergarten, then astonishing us with rabbinic interpretations of ensuing paragraphs. I heard the murmurs of four-year-old Ruthie and her friend Hillel, too young for the discussion, playing under the table during our last Milwaukee seder. I recalled taking a break from my kitchen preparations to see Julian poring over the Haggadah to prepare for the first time he led a seder. I saw him holding up the contemporary Haggadah we had purchased in Israel, pointing to the depiction of the four sons: the wise son as a scholar, the wicked son as an Israeli pioneer who forswore the prayer book for a shovel, the innocent son as a refugee from Europe, and the "one who does not know how to ask" as a Yemenite immigrant. I remembered annual reinterpretations of the four sons as our Haggadah collection grew and we had more artistic insights—and parental experience—to draw from. I heard our children's explanations of the rabbinic commentary that constitutes a large portion of the traditional Haggadah.

I remembered with an emotional shiver the insights into liberty and tyranny the year our guests included newly arrived Russian immigrants and a Holocaust survivor. I thought of seders with close friends and others with near strangers, with traditional and unobservant Jews, with college students and with Christian friends, all enriching the discussion.

"Our seders have been known to go on for six hours," I told Dad. I heard his sharp intake of breath. "Depending on who's at the table, we might talk about what the ancient words mean to us today, or what the rabbis meant in their time, textual interpretation suggested by an illustrator's rendition of the Haggadah, or almost anything. But don't worry," I reassured him, "Michael will adjust to his guests. Just eat ahead of time."

Dad reported later that it had been an interesting evening. He and Martha had left at midnight after consuming Miriam's delicious dinner.

"But we left before 'Who Knows One?' and 'An Only Kid,'" he grumbled.

I understood that the seder felt incomplete without these concluding songs. By now I had healed enough to return to my earlier love for this final part of the seder—especially Julian's barks, meows, moooos and thunk-thunks accompanying "An Only Kid." But they were no longer the crux. The warm, festive seders of my childhood had given way to celebrations that embraced the breadth and depth of Jewish tradition. Our leisurely pace through the Haggadah, with meanderings that varied according to the guests and the year, evoked deeper meanings and connections.

One such connection is to the line I had heard since childhood, "In every generation, it is incumbent upon each person to see himself as if he came forth out of Egypt." Our seder deliberations had helped me understand that I was among the multitudes that left Egypt and stood together at Sinai. I stood there, and so did my husband, our children, and our grandchildren, as well as our ancestors. On any given day, I might or might not believe that God acts in history and cares about me as an individual. But that day, as every day, I was convinced that I was part of whatever went on in that desolate, God-infused desert.

69

In May 1999, Julian and I were in Los Angeles for my sixtieth birthday. I could tell as we approached the table for Shabbat dinner that something was afoot. I expected a handmade gift or scribble from four-year-old Leah or perhaps a token from Miriam and Michael. Instead, Julian stood, opened a small book of Shabbat prayers, turned to me, and began to sing *Eshet Hayil,* A Woman of Valor, the lines from Proverbs with which a husband traditionally praises his wife. In all our years together, Julian had never said them to me in any language. And now he was stumbling through them in Hebrew, adoration lighting his face.

"A good wife, who can find? She is more precious than rubies.
Her husband places his trust in her and only profits thereby.
She brings him good, not harm, all the days of her life."

I sat transfixed by the scene. The hurt from my husband's years of cutting remarks, uttered from the depths of depression, began to melt away. This new Julian, reaching out to me with devotion, was the payoff for the years I had clung stubbornly to a marriage that often had felt pointless. Over the decades, he had given me jewelry, some handcrafted, some studded with diamonds and gems. But this testament to his love and admiration outshone them all; it was more precious to me than rubies. What a long road we had traveled together in the eighteen years since Ruth's death.

70

On that trip, Julian met our infant granddaughter, Kinneret, for the first time. I had been in Los Angeles three months before to care for Leah when Miriam gave birth. Back then, in February, Dad had asked, "Kinneret? What kind of name is that?"

"It's from the same Hebrew root as the word for violin. It means she's going to make beautiful music." The explanation had pacified my conventional father.

A bare year later, in April 2000, Aviva Ruth was born. Michael, superstitiously concerned about naming a baby for someone who had died so young, checked with his rabbi. "Aviva Ruth? And the Aviva is for her great-grandmother Anne, who lived into her nineties? No worry," his rabbi assured him. "The name takes us from *Hag Aviv,* the spring festival of Passover, to Shavuot, the holiday when we read the book of Ruth. It's perfect."

I was thrilled that my new granddaughter bore Ruth's name and wondered how she would be like her aunt. I hoped she would skip the tantrums but reflect Ruth's loving nature and Jewish commitment.

Mother's Day found me in Atlanta acquiring a new mother. After dating Martha for the ten years since Mom's death, Dad finally had convinced her to marry him. With joy, I witnessed and signed the ketubah for my 91-year-old father and his 79-year-old bride. I thought back thirty-nine years to my wedding. Not only did a ketubah play no part; I had never even heard of one. Chalk one up for Reform Judaism's rediscovery of lost traditions, I thought. And chalk up another for the egalitarianism that accepted my signature. Although I couldn't imagine trading the richness of my life today for the Reform Judaism of my childhood, some aspects still appealed.

The warm, simple marriage ceremony in Martha's living room may have solved one set of Dad's heart problems but not the physical ones. Alas, only two weeks later he called from the hospital to tell me that doctors had just installed a pacemaker. Down to Atlanta I flew again, and, as I would do numerous times in the coming months, helped him return to his own home. He had already outlived all the males in his family (as he had often told me), and seemed to feel that his end was approaching. Even the loving concern of his new wife didn't seem to cheer him.

Sitting next to him on his bed I said, "You know, Dad, you've always been my hero. I can't imagine my life without you. But I remember years ago, when you came to Smith for Father's Weekend, you told me that you believed a father owed his children three things: love, a good heritage, and an education. You've given me all of those, and more, and I'll be all right without you. I'll miss you terribly, but you have my permission to let go when you need to."

He sighed. "It's not so easy to let go."

71

That summer, Julian and I vacationed, as usual, in New York's Adirondack Park. As a child I had spent hours playing in the woods behind my house. At the Maine camp I attended for six years, canoeing and overnight camping had been my favorite activities. Forests, lakes, and rivers energized me, gave me serenity, and seemed to connect me with the Divine. I taught Julian to paddle, and we introduced our children to tent camping before they were a year old. After Miriam left for college, Julian and I discovered Timberlock, an unpretentious Adirondack resort. We returned summer after summer, always wishing we had found it when our children were young.

Our first few vacations there, we lit Shabbat candles on the dining porch amid the other guests, with Julian reciting kiddush quietly to me. This felt problematic, partly because the sun still shone brightly, but more because among the guests were other Jews—even a rabbi one year—who seemed embarrassed by our overt observance. We had to find a way that felt less awkward yet filled our need to celebrate Shabbat wherever we happened to be. A Friday evening in July 2000 was typical of the pattern we developed.

We joined all the guests for 6:30 dinner on the lodge's dining porch. At dusk, we walked to our lakefront cabin, which had neither electricity nor running water. We lit a small kerosene lamp so we could see to go to bed when the time came. I placed my candles in the tin washbasin for safety and lit them. We sat on the front porch and remarked on the single cloud, backlit by the rising moon. Julian said kiddush. Leaning over the porch rail, we dribbled moisture from a water bottle over our hands and said the appropriate blessing. On the arm of an Adirondack chair sat our challah rolls from home, wrapped in a red bandana. Julian held them up, recited the blessing, and sprinkled them with salt from a miniature Morton's container. We then ate "Shabbat dinner," challah and raspberries grown in our garden. After singing birkat hamazon, the blessing after the meal, we watched the last shadows disappear into the lake, the stillness interrupted only by rustling leaves, the darkness broken by the moon inching over the top of a cloud, until, full and refulgent, it reflected a shimmering path across Indian Lake. We savored a few minutes of Shabbat peace, grateful to be sitting outside in this incredible setting, before we picked our way along the wooded trail by a chemical light stick's greenish glow. At the lodge, we read until bedtime.

Typically, the next morning after breakfast, I sat near the lakeshore to pray the Shabbat service. When I arrived at the Amidah, a prayer said standing, I stepped onto a rock surrounded by water. Balancing carefully, I continued to pray. In the synagogue, this prayer would be followed by the Torah service and the rabbi's sermon. I gazed at the gentle ripples, gradually raising my eyes to take in the green trees and distant mountains sparkling in sunlight. "Such a serene spot," I said aloud to my congregation of rocks, water, trees, and a passing gull. "If only everyone in the world could experience such beauty, perhaps the world would know peace." I soaked in the splendor. Finally, still balanced on the rock, I glanced down at my prayer book and resumed my private service.

One Shabbat, just as I reached the concluding lines, I heard Julian stage-whisper, "B.J." I wondered why he was calling me when he could observe what I was doing. I uttered the final words, then looked up to see him in a canoe bracketed by two loons. We love the gorgeous black and white water birds with their haunting cry. One of our greatest pleasures is spotting loons on various Adirondack ponds. And he had managed to usher two to my chapel. As if in answer to my unspoken prayer. As if to emphasize God's wondrous presence. No synagogue service could ever compete.

72

Back in Rochester that summer of 2000, reality returned. Concerned about Dad's health, I called Margaret.

"Let's do Thanksgiving in Rochester this year," I suggested to my sister. "Do you think your older boys would come?"

"You can count on George and me, and Aaron. I hope Dan and Jon will, but I don't know."

After convincing Dad that he and Martha should fly to Rochester, I emailed all his descendants. When they heard that Granddad would be there, they all accepted. As the days grew shorter and colder, Dad wasn't sure he was well enough to travel. I called my sister again.

"What if he dies in Rochester?" we asked each other.

"Then he'd go with his boots on," we agreed. "He'd be surrounded by all his family. What could be better?"

At the last minute, Dad almost didn't come. "But you have to," I persuaded. "You're the reason that everyone else is making the trip." Later he told me that he had finally decided that if he lived even a few more weeks or months, he'd kick himself for having missed this chance to be with his children, grandchildren, and great-grandchildren.

When I saw how my dad, Joe, beamed when he held his namesake, Joey, born six weeks earlier to Eve and Larry, I knew I had been right to insist. All told, twenty-seven of us—including infants, a fiancée and a girlfriend—paid homage to Dad's greatest values: family cohesion and love. I was delighted with how well we respected each other's eating preferences (kosher, vegetarian, and no restrictions), Shabbat observance ("Do what you want in your room, but please don't turn off lights in public spaces that we can't turn back on"), and differences in lifestyle.

At Thanksgiving dinner, the youngest generation gave thanks for best friends and toys. The grandchildren, however, were acutely aware that they might never see their grandfather again.

"I'm thankful to be here with all my family and especially with Granddad."

"I'm happy that I've had Granddad in my life for so long."

"I'm thankful that Martha has brought so much happiness into Granddad's life."

"I'm grateful for Granddad's love and generosity."

Dad wiped his eyes, tried to speak, and gave an embarrassed grin instead. We didn't need words to appreciate his loving gratitude.

73

Julian and I signed up for a trip to Peru in February 2001. On one of my visits to Atlanta, I shared the itinerary with Dad and Martha. While Martha asked detailed questions about places we'd visit, Dad sat brooding. Finally, he spoke up. "What are the dates? When will you return? I hope I don't ruin it for you."

Once he had broached the subject, I felt free to tease him about it. "Dad, you wouldn't dare! I'll kill you if we get called back because you've up and died."

A few weeks later, Julian and I flew from Rochester to Miami, where we would connect with the Lima flight. We had ordered kosher meals, which turned out to be mushy eggs, a starchy side dish, and a fruit cup overpowered by sour grapefruit. I gazed enviously at the non-kosher meal being eaten by the passenger to my right: bagels and cream cheese. Only in America!

We arrived in Lima late at night and fell into bed at a charming pension. The next day began our tour, Overseas Adventure Travel's Affordable Peru. At the welcome dinner Thursday night, Julian and I passed by one dish after another on the laden buffet table.

"Does this have *carne,* meat?" we asked our guide.

"Yes."

"And this?"

"Not meat. Chicken."

"We can't eat that either.

"Are the beans made with lard?"

"Yes."

We tried to smile as we heaped our plates with rice.

"Only rice?" asked our guide, Juan Carlos. "We planned this dinner to include traditional foods."

"We told the travel company that we need vegetarian meals."

"Sorry," he said. "Tell me your requirements and I'll take care of it."

By the time we landed at 11,000-feet-high Cuzco the next day, we had bonded with our thirteen travel companions. As we drove along the Urubamba River in the Sacred Valley, I gazed up the steep green hills, amazed to see dots that actually were farmers working the nearly vertical slopes. At the massive Inca fortress of Ollantaytambo, where the Incan army routed an invasion in a rare defeat of Spanish forces, we climbed up huge terraces guarding the hilltop temple area. While we got our first lesson in Incan religion, I thought about the approaching Shabbat, and wondered how best to handle candle-lighting and kiddush.

I lit my candles at the appropriate time in our room at the Incaland Hotel. Then we met the group for cocktails. We compared reactions to the day's adventures. When there was a lull in the conversation, I spoke up.

"Julian and I have something to share with the group."

Everyone turned toward me, expectantly. "Tonight is our Sabbath. The Jewish day runs from sundown to sundown, so we begin the Sabbath in the evening with a ritual that includes lighting candles, which I did already in our room. Then Julian says a blessing that relates the Sabbath to creation and to the exodus from Egypt and praises God for creating wine. After that, we say another blessing over bread. At home, we would say it over two braided loaves of bread. Here, we'll use whatever rolls are on the table."

To my surprise, our trip mates listened intently. I continued, "If we were at home, we'd be sharing this meal and ritual with our family and friends. On this trip," I let my gaze move from one to the other, "you are our family. We hope you'll join us—though you'll be on your own to grab your own roll."

Our traveling companions smiled, nodded, and expressed their interest in learning more. Julian and I beamed at the warm responses.

When we had planned the Peru trip, Julian and I had considered looking for a kosher tour company. But we preferred not to limit our travel to strictly Jewish groups. We found that our compromise of traveling as vegetarians created opportunities to share Judaism with our travel companions. The opportunity for moments like these confirmed that we had chosen wisely.

"I'd like to sit with you at dinner," said Frank. "Maybe you can answer some of my questions about first-century Judaism."

A few minutes later, we arranged ourselves around a long table in the hotel dining room. Frank and his wife chose seats across from Julian and me. Everyone looked at Julian expectantly. He poured wine from the bottle he had purchased, raised his glass, and recited in Hebrew, followed by the English translation:

"And it was evening and it was morning, the sixth day. The heavens and the earth were finished, with all their array. On the seventh day God finished the work that He had been doing, and He ceased on the seventh day from all the work that He had done. And God blessed the seventh day and declared it holy…Blessed are you, Lord our God, sovereign of the world, creator of the fruit of the earth…."

The dining room seemed hushed as Julian passed wine to our temporary family. Lifting two rolls from the table, he blessed God "who brings forth bread from the earth."

"Do you think that Jesus recited the same blessings for the Sabbath that you just did?" Frank asked us.

"I've never thought about it, but it's quite likely," Julian said. "After all, the words of the kiddush are right out of Genesis, which Jesus would have known."

As we munched the vegetarian dinner that true to his word, Juan Carlos had arranged, Frank guided our discussion toward the Pharisees, a first century Jewish sect whose members were noted for strict observance of rites and rituals unrelated to the spirit or meaning of the ceremony. "It's obvious that you're not Pharisees. This really means something to you."

Over the next 24 hours, virtually everyone thanked us for including them in our Sabbath celebration. These rituals, which my parents and grandparents had rejected as separating them from the larger community, brought us closer to our gentile traveling companions. This came as no surprise. Over the years, Julian and I had found that our Christian colleagues and friends respected our adherence to tradition. Any negative reactions came, invariably, from less observant Jews. Did they feel threatened? Did they resent the "inconvenience" when we wouldn't answer the phone on Shabbat? Were they offended when we wouldn't eat meat products in their homes? Or did they just think us strange? I always called myself the "black sheep" of the family, but never took my self-deprecating description seriously because I knew, beyond doubt, that my family bond was too strong to be frayed by my religious practices.

At the end of one long day of touring, I leaned on the railing outside our hotel room and gazed west at the pink, orange, and golden sky. All day the date had haunted me: February 18, 2001, exactly 20 years since Ruth's death. Travel was a distraction but couldn't disguise the hole that had felt especially jagged during that day's adventures. In general, striking sunsets soothed my soul, but this sunset made me long for Ruth. How could one world hold so much beauty, so much hurt, so much goodness, and so much hardship? I had learned to live with the nagging loneliness the way one learns to live with a bad back—until a wrong step or a sudden turn wrenches the dull ache into acute pain.

My longing must have shown on my face. A trip mate strolling past paused. "Is something wrong?"

I shook my head, not wanting to explain, and she walked on. Oh Ruth, I thought. Why, why, why? Quashing the unanswerable questions, I returned to our room.

We spent our last few days in Peru along the Amazon and Napo Rivers. At the primitive lodges, which had the cleanest pit toilets I've encountered anywhere, I made good use of my one Spanish phrase.

"Sin carne?" I asked the staff at every meal.

"*Sin carne.*"

As I heaped my plate with rice and beans—the only possible choice—I hoped that Juan Carlos had indeed explained our needs and that I could trust the reply.

When we landed at the Miami airport after two stimulating weeks of travel, I hurried to call Dad.

"Thank God you're back."

He hadn't ruined our trip, but two weeks later came Martha's call that Dad was hemorrhaging, my hasty trip to his bedside, and his question, "Will you come back, even if it's after your Shabbat?"

"Y'know, Dad," I had responded. "There's commandment number four and there's number five. Next week, I'll be able to keep Shabbat, but I won't be able to honor you in person. I'll be back." I had kissed him and led Martha from the room.

When Martha and I reached Dad's house, my childhood home, her pace was agonizingly leisurely. Dad expected me to bring her back to the hospital, and she insisted on eating first. As the sun set over the backyard trees, I threw together supper for the two of us and lit my Shabbat candles. Minutes after we sat down at the breakfast room table, the phone rang.

"It's all over," Margaret said.

I responded with the traditional Jewish words, "*Baruch dayan emet,*" blessed be the Judge of truth.

My final words to Dad had been my promise to put my love and respect for him first. As I drove Martha back to the hospital, I reflected that even though he wouldn't know it, I was keeping my promise. I was heartbroken to lose the man whose love had enveloped me, whose balanced advice I respected, and whose sense of humor delighted us both. Nonetheless, I was at peace. And hopeful that Dad would give the promised hug to Ruth.

74

I have friends who would find fault with my decision to go back to the hospital on Shabbat, especially once I knew Dad already had died. Other friends wouldn't understand why this was a problem at all. My sister suggests that I am still a Reform Jew, but that today I sit in an Orthodox room. She may be right. All Jews make choices about whether or how much to observe, even those who attempt to do everything. As my son once suggested, observant Jews decide how much time to spend on which mitzvah. My fundamental choice has been to acknowledge that I am on a ladder with another rung to reach for. Sometimes my hold on a particular rung is precarious as I seek to balance the ritual and ethical sides of Judaism.

Both are as necessary to my life as every item on a seder plate is to the seder's ritual. In this complex life, opposite facets often join together to create the whole. I see these complementary forces in the seder plate's symbols: through my eyes, each has elements of both the bitter and the sweet. The roasted egg, for example, represents the festival offering made by pilgrims to Jerusalem in ancient days, a time of communal joy and a positive connection with our past. On the other hand, although I do not remember what I ate at the time, I am sure that eggs were served us at the first meal after Ruth's funeral, a reminder that life is a cycle, birth followed by death followed by another birth.

Karpas, a spring vegetable, symbolizes earth's renewal. Before we eat it, we dip it in salt water. Had I collected all my tears over the years, I would be prepared for every seder from now until the end of time.

Charoset, a sweet mixture, reminds us of the bricks and mortar made by Hebrew slaves in Egypt. Wistful memories of making charoset with Ruth blend with joyful recollections of preparing it with Miriam and more recently with my granddaughters.

Sometime in the 1970s, I acquired my first seder plate to hold the ritual foods. I was puzzled by what seemed to me to be an extra container. Apparently, there were two spots for *maror* or bitter herbs. At first I put grated horseradish in one, sliced horseradish in the other. Then

Larry asked me to use romaine lettuce because he needed to eat a certain amount to meet the rabbinic requirements and he couldn't handle that much horseradish. Lettuce, he said, was an acceptable substitute. Still, I didn't understand the reason for two types of bitter herbs.

Only in the context of my own struggles do I finally comprehend. Bitterness has come to me in different degrees and flavors. There was the childhood devastation of losing my best friend because her "parents said so," the resentment of being singled out in class for being Jewish and not believing in Jesus, and the humiliation in the French synagogue created by my own appalling ignorance. Worse were my mother's illness and my sister's death. All of these hurt, but they didn't stop my life. They were like Larry's lettuce—a bitter herb someone could eat in quantity and still be able to handle.

Ruth's death, on the other hand, was like swallowing a tablespoon of fresh, undiluted horseradish in one bite: raw, stinging, can't-breathe, can't-stem-the-tears, don't-want-to-go-on-living bitterness. This maror's texture and long-term effects were qualitatively different from the bitterness represented by lettuce.

The final item on the seder plate is a lamb shank, *zeroa,* that represents the lamb that the Hebrews slaughtered on the night that God imposed the tenth plague, the death of firstborn Egyptians. The Israelites were commanded to mark their doorposts with the lamb's blood so the angel of death would pass over their homes, then they were to roast and eat the lamb with bitter herbs. In Hebrew, the word zeroa also means "upper arm." Thus, zeroa refers not only to the paschal lamb but also to the "strong arm of God" that brought us out of Egypt.

Where was God's arm, I wonder, to stop the drunk driver that Sabbath eve in Utica? If we are all in God's pocket, as Orthodox Jews often claim, then was Ruth's death an enactment of the divine will? The rabbis tell us that to save one life is to save the world. If the Supreme Being is, as tradition also suggests, both omnipotent and merciful, then why didn't God stretch out those divine hands to steer the car and save the world? Couldn't God have overridden the driver's free will? These are tough questions that I try not to ask too often because I have learned that no answers will satisfy me or fill the Ruth-shaped hole in my heart.

Perhaps this is why the Hagaddah gives no explicit answers to the four questions asked traditionally by the youngest at the table: to prepare us for the fact that life's most profound puzzles have no ready solutions.

We read in the Bible's first verses that before creation the earth was *tohu vavohu*, without form and void. The universe was dark, disturbed by a sweeping wind. "God said, 'Let there be light,' and thus began the orderly process of creation. Darkness and unsettling thoughts overwhelmed me in the chaotic days and months after Ruth's death. I had had no control over my child's life and death, and what else mattered? What light broke through came from my other children and my friends and from the structure of traditional Judaism. I found comfort in each new step up the ladder, partly from identifying with Ruth's life, partly because the boundaries brought order to a life that felt out of control.

Today when the questions intrude on my mostly orderly life, I remember my friend Esther's words: "Of course I question God. How can a thinking person not raise questions? The difference is that I never stop following the mitzvot, even when I question." Back then, I listened and kept questioning; today, I try to limit my doubts and keep climbing.

I often have asked myself what my life would be like had Julian and I never moved from Atlanta. Much as I would have loved for my children to have more frequent contact with their grandparents and other relatives, I suspect I would have had more trouble becoming my own person. I might never have braved my parents' and my in-laws' displeasure by sending my children to a Jewish day school. I might have found Shabbat too inconvenient, kashrut too restrictive. I most likely would never have heard that black-garbed rabbi talk about the ladder of tradition, an image that has challenged and pulled me upward for more than forty years. And I might never have met kind, loving Orthodox Jews like Helen and the Klitsners, whose outstretched arms embraced me and supported my hesitant first steps.

A friend recently queried, "Shouldn't Yom Kippur, the Day of Atonement, precede Rosh Hashanah, the New Year, so that we start the year with a clean slate?" Then, with a laugh, she answered her own question. "It's so Jewish! We take who we are with us, even as we enter a fresh year. We can improve ourselves, but we can't discard who we are. We can't get rid of our past."

My friend's insight resonates with my thoughts as I conclude this memoir. In my seventies, I am still the little girl who wants to please her parents, do well in school, and have fun with friends. I have not discarded the teenager who enjoyed religious services, loved to paddle a canoe and play in the woods, and took seriously the prophet Micah's words to "do justly, love mercy, and walk humbly with God." I'm still married to the guy I met at a Jewish event when I was sixteen. And, despite a loving family, good friends, and a place in my community, I always feel a little like an outsider.

The little girl who grew up in a fairy-tale world, with only occasional dragons to spew bitterness, could never have imagined my daily longing for Ruth. Although Ruth no longer occupies my first and last thoughts of the day, she is never far from my consciousness. What would she be doing today? Would she be married? Have children? Would she be a teacher? A social worker? Perhaps even a rabbi? It's hard to imagine a forever-thirteen-year-old in her forties, but I can't help trying.

How do I go on? The same way I moved from my liberal Jewish childhood to my current life: one faltering step at a time. Traditional Judaism, especially its structure and strong sense of community, gives me the strength to face each day and even to find joy in its celebrations. My greatest delights come from the blessings of my two living children and their children. And when all else fails, a paddle in my solo canoe—my favorite way to experience God's natural world—is guaranteed to bring a smile to my face and a sense of gratitude to my heart.

75

2009

Julian and I beam from opposite ends of the table. Children and grandchildren range on either side, cousins vying to sit near cousins they rarely see. We have each selected a Haggadah from a wide selection collected over the years, some with interesting commentary, others with beautiful illustrations. The younger children hold the ones they made in school. Julian's red and yellow paperback edition is wine-stained, dog-eared, and dotted with handwritten notes that reflect his thoughts as leader through the years. In it he has also recorded the names of our guests, or hosts, for every seder since 1974.

"What do we do first?" he asks. "Who knows the order of the seder?"

"I do! I do!" calls out Calanit, at five our youngest grandchild.

"Can you sing it?" prompts Grandpa.

Her cousin Ruthie, seven, a born performer, starts in a high voice. "Kadesh, urhatz…" We all join her to chant the order of the Passover seder.

We pour wine or grape juice for each other—free people never pour their own—and recite kiddush. I picture Joey two years ago, when Larry asked his then-six-year-old son to read the Hebrew. Joey complied, we said "amen" and drank our wine. Joey looked up in surprise, "Did I just say kiddush?" Now he, and all his siblings and cousins, read Hebrew more fluently than their grandparents, though I continue to study and struggle to conquer the language.

This has to be one of the longest seders ever. "What is there to discuss?" my father once asked. Let's see: Why do we wash our hands without saying a blessing? Why do we eat a green vegetable? Why did my family use parsley and Julian's use potatoes? Why is the phrase "All who are hungry—let them come and eat," written in Aramaic, not Hebrew? To every question, someone has an answer, and often another question as well. The children pipe up with interpretations they learned in their Jewish day schools in New Jersey and California. The teenagers give more thoughtful interpretations, ask more sophisticated questions. "What is the relationship between law and freedom?" "Suppose the Exodus had never happened…would we be Jewish today?" "Why do the men get all the credit?"

I think of my father's question—which is more important, honoring your parents or keeping Shabbat?—and am grateful that these grandchildren seem to take seriously both the ethical and the ritual sides of Judaism. Only time will tell how they will balance them and how they will respond intellectually and spiritually to their birthright.

We recite the ten plagues, using our pinkie fingers or a knife to spill a drop of wine or grape juice for each plague. Sam, fifteen, explains, "This symbolizes our sadness at the loss of human life, even our enemies'. We can't be totally happy about the plagues when we know that so many Egyptians died when they followed the Israelites into the sea."

"That's right," his sister Ariella agrees. "We don't rejoice in others' misfortune, even when it helps us."

And, a few pages, later, "How thankful must we be to God, the All-Present, for all the good He did for us." We sing in rousing Hebrew:

"Had He brought us out from Egypt
And not executed judgment against them,
Di-ayenu, It would have been enough for us!"

Multiple verses later, we conclude,

"Had He brought us to the Land of Israel
And not built for us the Holy Temple,
Di-aynu, It would have been enough for us!
Di-di-aynu, Di-aynu, Di-ay-nu!"

Finally, we are ready for the festive meal. Miriam, Eve, and the older girls help me serve okra soup for the vegetarians as well as traditional chicken soup, brisket and turkey, matzah farfel stuffing, carrots, asparagus, and salad.

"Whoever says there are no good desserts during Pesach hasn't tasted Grandma's baking," Yael says.

"All your wonderful assistance makes them even better." Preparing a seder with my grandchildren's help is this Grandma's dream.

It is eight years since Dad died. For Julian's 70th Passover, he wanted to have a "Zaidy (Grandpa) Seder." We have brought all the children and grandchildren to Rochester for a joint celebration of his past November birthday and mine next month in May. We all miss Leah, Miriam's eldest, whose father refused to release her from her court-ordered obligation to spend every Pesach with him. Not even Julian's personal request for three days out of ten swayed him.

For me, the high point of this week together comes at lunch the second day, when Miriam says to the children, "You know, we're not just three generations in this room."

"We're not?" asks Kinneret, ten.

"In the picture behind me is my great-great…how many greats, Mom?"

"That woman in the astounding Bavarian headdress is my great-great-great-grandmother, so four greats for you," I reply.

Miriam points to another portrait. "And over there is Granny, my great-

grandmother."

"You were so lucky to know your great-grandmother!" Aviva, nine, chimes in.

"Yes," agrees Miriam. "She lived 'til 103. I was eleven when she died, so I have very clear memories of her." Miriam gestures toward a painting of an old French peasant woman holding a seder plate with the same symbols we have cherished this week. "And that lady isn't a relative. But from the time I was your age, I've seen her as offering me the tradition. I wouldn't dare not accept it."

I had no idea that Miriam felt that way about my seder lady. When my daughter was an infant, I had seen the portrait hanging in my Seattle aunt's front hall. "Some day, may you live to 120, I'd love to have that," I had unsubtly hinted.

"Sorry, but it's already promised."

When, after my uncle's death in 1977, Aunt Emilie called to tell me the seder lady was on her way to Rochester, I thanked her profusely, but never thought to ask what had changed. I love this work by Alfonse Levy, who, like my great-grandfather, was from Alsace-Lorraine. The territory, on the French-German border, went back and forth between the two countries. It was French during the period between my great-grandfather Moses Blum's birth in 1830 and his emigration to America in 1849.

"Did you know that the artist did a whole series of these Alsatian peasants to preserve at least a memory of the Jewish customs that he assumed were disappearing?" I ask Miriam.

"I guess we're proving him wrong—aren't we, kids?"

As my grandchildren nod their acceptance of the tradition I have climbed rung by rung to reclaim, I look up at the portrait of Granny, Moses Blum's daughter. Thank you for saving my place in the Jewish people. If you hadn't maintained at least social ties to Judaism, where would I be today? Probably not at a Pesach table, surrounded by grandchildren who assume traditional Judaism as their natural heritage.

That evening, Miriam, Eve, and I light Shabbat candles together. With outstretched hands, we circle the flames three times, cover our faces, and bless God "who commanded us to light the Sabbath candles." Then, as Miriam and Eve turn to bless their children, I pray silently.

"Baruch ata Adonai Eloheinu, Melekh ha'olam, shehekianu, v'kimanu, v'higianu lazman hazeh. *Thank you, God, for keeping me alive, sustaining me, and enabling me to reach this season.*"

Glossary

aliyah — the honor of being called up to say the blessings on passage chanted from the Torah scroll

bar mitzvah — a ceremony and celebration for a Jewish boy on his 13th birthday when he takes on the religious duties and responsibilities of an adult

bat mitzvah — a ceremony and celebration for a Jewish girl on her 12th or 13th birthday when she takes on the religious duties and responsibilities of an adult

briss — the Jewish circumcision ceremony where a baby boy is entered into the covenant of Abraham

challah — an egg-rich bread that is usually braided or twisted before baking and is traditionally eaten by Jews on the Sabbath and holidays

charoset — a mixture of apples, nuts, and cinnamon that represents the clay the Hebrew slaves used to make bricks, served as part of the Passover seder

chavurah — a small group of like-minded Jews who assemble for the purposes of facilitating Shabbat and holiday prayer services and sharing communal experiences

chuppah — marriage canopy

d'var Torah — "word of Torah," or sermon

get — Jewish divorce document

haggadah — the book of readings for the seder service

halachah — Jewish law

Hallel — a set of psalms that are part of the liturgy on holidays, new moons, and the Passover seder

hamentaschen — triangular pastries that are traditional Purim treats

Kaddish — a prayer praising God, particularly recited by mourners and those observing yahrzeit

kasher — to purify an item previously used for non-kosher food

kashrut — the rules and practice of eating kosher food

ketubah — Jewish marriage contract

kiddush — the prayer, recited over a cup of wine or grape juice, that begins the Sabbath or holiday
kipa — a skull cap, worn to symbolize awareness of God's presence
kosher — accepted by Jewish law as fit for eating or drinking
kvell — to be extraordinarily proud
mazel tov — congratulations
mechitza — the divider separating the women's section from the men's in an Orthodox synagogue
menorah — an object that holds seven or nine candles and that is used in Jewish worship
mishloach manot — gifts of food exchanged on the holiday of Purim
mitzvah — religious commandment
mitzvot — plural of mitzvah; the Divine commandments of Judaism
mohel — a person who performs ritual Jewish circumcisions
Pesach — Passover
rebbitzen — a rabbi's wife
refusenik — a Jew living in the Soviet Union who was refused permission to emigrate
Rosh Hodesh — the new moon, which marks the start of the Hebrew month
seder — the ritual meal and service, held on the first and second evenings of Passover, recalling the exodus of the Jews from Egypt
shammash — the candle on the hanukkah menorah that lights the other candles
Shavuot — the holiday marking the giving of the Torah
shiva — the seven-day mourning period following the funeral
Shmini Atzeret — the eighth day of Sukkot
shofar — the ram's horn blown on Rosh Hashanah and Yom Kippur
shtetl — a small Jewish town or village formerly found in Eastern Europe
Simhat Torah — the rejoicing of the law, celebrates the completion of the annual cycle of reading the Torah
sukkah — a booth or shelter with a roof of branches and leaves that is used especially for meals during Sukkot
Sukkot — a fall holiday

Talmud — The central text of post-Biblical Judaism, collecting rabbinic teachings and discussions and compiled around the year 500

traif — non kosher.

tzitzit — ritual fringes

yahrzeit — the anniversary of a death

yarmulke — skull cap

yeshiva — a Jewish school for religious instruction

z"l — an abbreviation for *zichrona l'vracha*, may her memory be a blessing

Acknowledgements

This memoir began not as an idea for a book but as a simple response to an exercise in Sonja Livingston's Creative Nonfiction class at Rochester's Writers & Books. Over time, it became the subject of most of my writing in Anais Salibian's Memoir class. My wonderful classmates, who became dear friends, read it with rigor and devotion, as I wrote, revised, and polished some more. Thanks to Joanna Hodgman, Dia Lawrence, Elaine Miller, Joy Nimick, Suzanne Schnittman, Dottie Waldron, and Lois Welch *z"l*, my first and most critical readers.

Finally, after several years, I called on Susan Bono to read it with fresh eyes. She said what I had suspected: The structure did not support the weight of what was now a full-length book. She helped me find the right construction, and her innumerable, penetrating questions forced me to fill in the gaps. I couldn't have asked for a better reader and coach.

Lea Gavrieli's copy-editing clarified stories I told too tightly. Cali Lovett helped me make editorial choices in the final stages. Joanne Palmer gave it a final polish. My thanks to them all.

Throughout, Julian helped with specifics. I suspect he dreaded those times I walked into his study, saying, "Do you remember that night in Milwaukee when....?" He usually recalled the context but not the content, leaving me free to tell the story as I remembered it.

At last, with great trepidation, I handed him the entire manuscript. My goal had been truth, which meant I did not always show him in the best light, but I certainly tried to be fair. His reaction was totally positive. My children, Larry and Miriam, each made a few factual corrections, for which I am grateful. I thank them for enduring the painful parts of our family life and especially for growing into adults of whom I am immensely proud.

CPSIA information can be obtained at www.ICGtesting.com
Printed in the USA
BVOW03s0736251114

376584BV00006B/25/P